New Library of Pastoral Care

Crisis Counselling

New Library of Pastoral Care

NEW·LIBRARY·OF

PASTORAL·CARE

CRISIS
COUNSELLING

Caring for People in Emotional Shock

Revised Edition

Howard W. Stone

SPCK

Revised edition
first published in the United States of America 1993
This edition first published in Great Britain 1995
Society for Promoting Christian Knowledge
Holy Trinity Church
Marylebone Road
London NW1 4DU

© Augsburg Fortress 1993

Scripture quotations, unless otherwise noted, are from the
New Revised Standard Version of the Bible, copyright © 1989
by the Division of Christian Education of the National Council
of the Churches of Christ in the United States.

British Library Cataloguing-in-Publication Data

A catalogue record for this book is available
from the British Library

ISBN 0-281-04809-6

Typeset by Pioneer Associates, Perthshire
Printed in Great Britain by
The Cromwell Press, Melksham, Wilts.

For Karen and Christine

Contents

Foreword

The fact that the original edition of this book stayed in print for over sixteen years merits comment. The continuing appreciation to this book by ministers, seminarians, and a wide variety of crisis team members indicates how a succinct manual on crisis helping methods such as this is needed, both within and outside of religious settings. The books in this series are both practice-oriented and focused on particular problems that ministers—both ordained and lay—encounter regularly in working with burdened persons. Certainly no issues requiring caring and counseling skills occur more frequently or are more challenging than the variety of crises that Howard Stone explores.

This completely revised edition builds on and goes beyond the original edition in several ways. First, it includes an entirely new chapter (chap. 4) which illuminates a number of contemporary crises that are perplexing, demanding, and frequently exhausting when encountered even by experienced counselors. These include threatened suicide and homicide, sexual calls, and high-risk crises, such as volatile, often dangerous family fights which the author advises to avoid if possible. Drawing on his in-depth experience of doing crisis counseling over the years, Stone also offers important guidelines for protecting your personal safety in potentially hazardous situations.

Second, the principles and guidelines of crisis intervention described are made more concrete and understandable by the author's sprinkling the text with case vignettes. Many of these are from his own experiences as a pastoral counselor and so ring true.

Third, in addition to many brief case examples, Stone presents several cases in more depth. These show how to respond constructively to crises such as attempted suicide, Alzheimer's disease, job losses, and a child's reaction to a family's moving. The discussion of the multiple uses of the telephone in crisis care and counseling is potentially

1

invaluable to overloaded ministers, including the recommendations for handling both crank and prank phone calls. Stone's family systems and theological orientation are clearly evident throughout the book and are among its many strengths.

What a delight to write a foreword for an outstanding book by a former student who is also a long-time colleague and collaborator in professional projects. I must confess that a small part of me wishes that I could claim what Howard knows about crisis counseling as being learned from this former teacher. But, reality quickly interrupts this self-congratulatory fantasy. In reading this book, I become aware of both the riches of Howard Stone's self-taught knowledge regarding crisis counseling and the amount that a former teacher can learn from a former student.

In sum, I am delighted to recommend this book wholeheartedly. It is a valuable helping manual for anyone who seeks more workable answers to the painful crises in the lives of those with whom they walk as caring guides through shadowed valleys. The book will also be helpful to readers searching for ways to become more cope-able in their own dark valleys.

HOWARD CLINEBELL

Preface

Howard Clinebell had a present for me, as it was for him when he came across it. He had been lecturing in Taiwan, and his host presented him with a book—a Chinese version of *Crisis Counseling*! It had been translated by his interpreter, Kaofang Yeh, a graduate student in pastoral counseling from the School of Theology at Claremont. At that time, Taiwan did not subscribe to international copyright laws so the publisher had not been consulted—and neither Howard Clinebell nor I had any inkling of the existence of this Chinese edition.

Our surprise on discovering that book has been a continuing one for me: *Crisis Counseling* has been translated into five languages and has met a response I never expected.

I believe that this response results from a need—and a concern—that clergy and other pastoral caregivers feel with regard to the crisis situations they encounter. In most communities, the pastor is a key figure—often the first recourse—for people in crisis. When someone in a crisis arrives at the door, you are on the spot—needed and now. People in crisis rely on their pastor to know what to do, to steer them through emergency, tragedy, disaster, loss. Often they are paralyzed; it is up to you to help them get moving again.

It is a frightening experience. *Crisis Counseling* exists because of my own need and concerns in crisis situations. Before I attended graduate school, before I even had the idea of writing a book, I began collecting questions and reflections on people in crisis with whom I was meeting in ministry: what worked, what did not, how people acted, what I could read that would better prepare me for the next time.

Now, many years after the first publication of *Crisis Counseling,* a revised edition is needed: I have changed, some of my views have changed, and the field has changed. There has been new research. Students, colleagues, and counselees have asked questions, made suggestions, shared insights, and shaped my thinking. Above all, the times have changed. New or newly named diseases such as AIDS are spreading, and diseases like Alzheimer's have come to the fore. Crime has increased. People are living on the edge. No one is safe. Modern existence seems to be a crisis waiting to happen.

What began as a face-lift of *Crisis Counseling,* therefore, became a thorough revision. Hardly a paragraph remains unchanged. I also made additions: chapter 4 is new; I added material on suicide, crisis counseling on the telephone, intervention in volatile or hazardous situations, and personal safety of the minister. A shift in focus may also be evident to readers familiar with the first edition. Although crisis intervention theory arose primarily from psychotherapeutic theory and practice involving the individual, this revised book places greater emphasis on marriage and family systems.

Crisis Counseling unites the historic skills of pastoral care and counseling with current methods of crisis intervention from the fields of psychology and psychotherapy. Like the original edition, the present book is written for ministers—both clergy and lay—who are called upon to care for those in crisis; its concepts and techniques will be of value to mental health professionals and crisis hot line volunteers as well. It discusses the minister's role as a crisis intervener and shares my understanding of recent crisis intervention theory. I urge the reader to give particular attention to chapter 2, because a thorough grasp of the dynamics of crisis is vital for effective crisis management.

Chapter 3 is the core of the book; it presents a detailed methodology of crisis intervention. Chapter 5 illustrates these techniques with case studies that demonstrate the wide variety of situations which benefit from crisis intervention methods. (All cases presented in this book, though modified to protect confidentiality, are taken from my own counseling ministry and that of other ministers and students.) Finally, chapter 6 addresses the whole community of faith and its role in offering care and support to people in their times of greatest need.

Some terms may require clarification. Although this book is titled *Crisis Counseling,* it might better fall under the heading of pastoral care; many of the crisis situations described need far more than a standard fifty-minute hour in the pastor's office. I use crisis counseling and crisis intervention interchangeably to include both pastoral counseling and pastoral care (a home visit, a typical counseling session, a telephone conversation, or even arranging for other people to do the helping). To identify the people involved, I make the following distinctions: *clergy* and *pastor* refer to ordained ministers, priests, and rabbis. *Minister, pastoral carer, helper,* and *caregiver* refer to laypersons as well as the ordained. The person in crisis is identified in a variety of ways, such as troubled person, person in distress, counselee, and parishioner. (I avoided the term "client," traditional to psychotherapy, because it seems less appropriate in pastoral situations.)

In this brief space I cannot adequately express appreciation to the many people who helped and influenced me in the development of *Crisis Counseling.* Nevertheless I would like to give my special thanks to John Landgraf, Alton Goodenberger, Herbert Anderson, Howard Clinebell, Brian Feille, and Timothy Staveteig for reading the manuscript and offering valuable suggestions. I am grateful to over twenty years of students for their enthusiam, questions, and contributions to my thinking. I also want to thank the military chaplains, especially the Navy chaplains, for helping to develop the ideas in chapter 4. To the readers of the first edition of *Crisis Counseling* who helped to shape this new edition by sending comments, criticism, and ideas—thank you and keep writing; I value your feedback. Finally, to Karen Stone, who helped prepare both versions of the manuscript, I can never fully express my gratitude . . . but I will surely try.

Introduction
to the British Edition

The *New Library of Pastoral Care* aims to assist people concerned with pastoral care, whether lay or ordained, to improve their knowledge and their skills. It is also hoped that it may prove useful to others who may wish to understand the role of the pastor and develop their understanding of pastoral care.

The title and format of Howard Stone's book suggest a genre which the British tend to associate with the United States and to disdain—'the how-to book'. Some of its assumptions—for instance, the reference to 'fifty minutes in the pastor's office'—seem far from the experience of the average British minister. They usually have no office and can rarely find fifty minutes. But crisis counselling itself is something about which all concerned with their pastoral care can usefully familiarise themselves.

Counselling itself is today being increasingly questioned. This doubt is part of a more widespread social concern about the value of therapy in general. A series of well-publicised scandals have created concern about therapy and therapeutically-informed social work. At the same time the churches have become more self-aware. They have consequently begun to re-examine their distinctive contribution in the field of pastoral care. This is no longer the prerogative of the churches. 'Pastoral care' and 'counselling', therefore, do not go so obviously together as once might have been assumed. The churches' primary discipline is once again being regarded as theology, albeit informed by contemporary psychological insights.

Crises have great attractions. They make all involved feel wanted and needed. They are, therefore, dangerous. A crisis-oriented approach could create delusions in counsellors and ministers alike about their importance. And no effective work can ever be done on the basis of delusion. But Howard Stone's clear analysis of the way that a crisis develops (page 19) should prevent this. His outline is a useful paradigm for many of the situations in which ministers, lay and ordained, find themselves. These encounters are marked by their occasional nature. Ministers report that their dealings with people are more fleeting than they used to be. A series of visits or meetings is the exception rather than the rule. The same is true of much social life. It is fragmentary and the meetings are brief. Someone turns to someone else for help, is assisted, and then the encounter ends, often altogether. The crisis is not presented fully for the pastor to handle. They have their own internal crisis about how to handle people in such fragmentary and brief meetings.

By comparison with the world which Stone describes relations between people in Great Britain are less intimate. The minister is not so likely to be known, either as pastor or friend, in so deep a sense. Some of the stories might appear awkward, although the content (divorce, family problems, suicide) is only too familiar. Their strangeness lies in the way in which the pastor is called in and involved. British ministers will find both the approach to them and the resulting intervention less direct and more fragmentary. The encounters are more one-off, although the way that such an encounter often leads tangentially to other indirect contacts should not be underestimated. This may, however, be one consequence of the different environment in which the American and British churches work. In both nations, so it appears, a religious force remains powerful. It has not been obliterated by the process of secularisation. But in the USA religion is practised more overtly. There is greater public association with churches. British society by contrast is less specifically Christian.

Because of this difference, however, and not in spite of it, this book is especially useful in clarifying many aspects of crisis encounter in Great Britain. Although a product of the United States, it is not so tied to the American scene that it cannot be understood. And because Stone writes from a religious context that is more overt than that prevailing in the United Kingdom, he exposes much that is happening covertly in Britain. The analysis of how a crisis develops, for example, can be applied to many situations. The tendency to take something at face value without analysing the process which brings it about is a dangerous simplification in any activity. In particular, study of this book will help secular helpers and lay and ordained ministers to become more alert to the veiled messages that may be being sent to them when they counsel anyone. It is not that everyone is in crisis, in Stone's technical sense. But to seek help has in this country something of the quality of a crisis itself.

For ministers in the British context there are three aspects of crisis counselling that need attention. First, even in Great Britain residual Christianity remains, even if it is largely ill-informed and inarticulate. But if people approach a Christian person, they expect Christian imagery and behaviour to be assumed. Possibly to some extent because this distinctive belief has sometimes been minimised, people have been disappointed when they have come to a minister. They seek a religious encounter, not a therapeutic intervention. Second, one aspect of this encounter which may be stronger in the UK than the USA is the ritual dimension. Among the resources available to the pastor is that of ritual. These become an explicit point of ministry in baptisms, weddings, and funerals. But there are also lesser rituals, some of which may even need devising with people as part of the act of ministering. And third, in a society in which Christianity is more residual than in Stone's world, the interpretative function of the minister, whether lay or ordained, may need more attention. This is implicit in Stone's approach but needs to be articulated by British ministers more coherently to themselves. The person in crisis is likely to be less clear about the framework in which he or she and the minister is working. The person offering help, therefore, will have to spend more time gently trying to discover the contractual basis of the meeting—i.e. what the person is here for. That requires the sort of empathy that Stone describes, but with the minister being more alert to the question of the role that he or she holds for the other.

In such a context, since pastoral ministry is theologically based, the minister will also need to work at creating a stronger theological grounding than Stone provides. Ministers will have to elaborate the final chapter on 'The Church as a Caring Community' according to the polity of their own church. The theological justification for ministry, especially with those who are avowedly and deliberately not members of the church, lies in an understanding of the church first, and only secondarily of what shape ministry should take. That is why the question of authority to minister, to which Stone gives some attention, is becoming more acute. The question of what the church is and for whom its ministry is available underlies all approaches to ministry and determines what form that ministry takes. It also determines the capacity of the church to deploy its ordained and lay resources in complementary fashion.

This book should assist many involved in any way in counselling people in crisis. It has the down-to-earth nature of a 'how-to' book, but is more thoughtful than that. If used with care, it provides a brief, accessible, and very useful approach to some important aspects of counselling and pastoring in today's context.

WESLEY CARR   *Bristol Cathedral*

This is the first publication in the *New Library of Pastoral Care* since I succeeded Derek Blows as Series Editor. This transition should not go unrecorded. The series is its own fine monument. Its overall quality, variety of topics, and unified (but not uniform) stance, are tributes to Derek Blows' generosity and skill as Editor.

ONE

The Minister as Crisis Counselor

I was working in my study early one Wednesday evening when I received a telephone call from Sandra Chase, a woman in the Philadelphia congregation where I was serving as assistant pastor.*

Sandra was nearly hysterical. She said she had to see me right away because her seventeen-year-old son Gary had just informed her that he was going to elope that weekend. She was passionately opposed to the youthful marriage, but Gary was equally adamant, and they wanted my help.

Before I had a chance to ask whether Sandra had called the senior pastor, she reminded me that he was out of town. I agreed to meet with Sandra, her husband Leonard, Gary, and his fiancée Jeanne later that evening.

This was the first crisis I had been called upon to deal with in the role of pastor. As I drove to the Chases' home, I felt fear: I knew other people were counting on me because I was a minister, but I did not have a clue about what to do.

Both teenagers seemed mature and were willing to talk. I had also called Jeanne's parents, but they indicated that they would not even speak with me. Sandra and Leonard finally decided to support the couple when they realized the wedding was going to take place with or without their approval. But they wanted a church wedding for their son. It was relatively easy to help the four reach a compromise on that point. After Gary and Jeanne returned from their elopement, the church's rite for

*All names have been changed and, as necessary, situations modified to protect the privacy of the individuals described.

the Blessing of a Civil Marriage, much like a wedding, was conducted with congregation, family, and friends sharing in the event.

The young couple came to me for several counseling sessions afterward, each time discussing where they would live, finances, sex, contraception, children, and how they would deal with relatives (especially her parents). Some bad feelings remained; the elder Chases were particularly resentful toward Jeanne's parents for "abandoning" the couple. But the church ceremony, and the willingness of most of the people involved to get together and talk, helped Jeanne and Gary start on a good foot at a time of life that can often be exceedingly hazardous. The successful resolution of this crisis may have helped them deal with future crises.

All of us experience crises from time to time. We reach an edge, an emergency, a moment arrives when a decision must be made, a problem solved, a significant issue dispatched, a terrifying or agonizing situation confronted. We are constrained to make elemental choices. Crises force us to recognize that we are unprotected and naked before others, God, and even ourselves. Indeed, Charles Gerkin (1979, 32-33) describes a crisis as an extreme or boundary condition in which

> the fundamental contradiction between human aspirations and finite possibilities becomes visible in such a way as to demand attention. In the situational crisis we are confronted with our human vulnerability, our finitude, the utter impossibility of our deepest hopes and wishes. In that situation a most elemental choice is forced upon persons that is at its core a religious or "faith" choice. Either persons must defend themselves against the contradiction with whatever human defense is possible, be that denial or heroic courage, or they must open themselves to the vulnerability of the unknown future, trusting in the power and care of God coming out of the change and contingency of the unknown.

In one way or another, whether ministers like it or not, they are faced with crises in people's lives. Crisis ministry has been part of pastoral care throughout many centuries; indeed, Christians have learned to expect their pastors to be with them at such times.

A literature and methodology referred to as "crisis intervention" has emerged since the 1940s in the fields of psychology, psychiatry, and social work. The purpose of this book is to blend learnings from these mental health fields with the skills of pastoral care. I will not survey various methods of crisis intervention practice, but rather share a particular method of intervention based upon recent theories of crisis—a method that has a broad theoretical base and has been effective in practice.

KEY CONCEPTS

A crisis can be understood as a crucial time and a turning point. In the present context it is the term for an individual's internal reaction to an external hazard. Involved is a temporary loss of coping abilities, a paralysis of action. Any definition of crisis makes a tacit assumption that the emotional dysfunction is reversible. Persons in crisis are not necessarily mentally ill, they are simply responding to a hazardous circumstance. If they effectively cope with the threat, a return to former levels of functioning will result.

Although this definition speaks of crisis as an internal reaction of an individual, one must not forget that crises also happen to families (Pittman 1987). When a crisis precipitated by some threatening external event comes to bear on a system (e.g., a family), it weakens the internal boundaries of the system, and that system is more open—not only vulnerable but also receptive—to help from the outside. Crises strike not only isolated individuals but also families, extended families, congregations, and systems great and small.

The two basic types of crisis are *developmental* and *situational*. Normal developmental crises are the predictable, though critical, experiences everyone goes through in the maturation process, such as the turmoil attendant upon adolescence or middle age (Erikson 1964). Situational crises are exceptional and unpredictable; they are the upheavals resulting from unusual circumstances such as divorce or a disabling accident.

The aim of pastoral crisis intervention—and the aim of this book— is to help individuals and families deal with the latter. Situational crises might arise in connection with the loss of a job, of a support person, or of a position of status and respect; an incapacitating accident, illness, or operation (such as a mastectomy); the death of a friend, child, or spouse; one's own impending death; the discovery of marital infidelity; retirement; an unwanted pregnancy; moving to a new city; learning that one is HIV positive; a national disaster or massive calamity such as war, hurricane, or an explosion; inheriting children from a previous marriage; abortion; arrest or incarceration; sudden religious conversion; miscarriage; premature birth; post-traumatic stress disorder (PTSD); birth of a less-than-perfect child; rape or incest; loss of welfare money; entering a retirement home; parents coming to live with their married children; a home burglary—the list could go on and on. Any event that poses a grave threat to a person or a family may precipitate a situational crisis.

Crisis intervention refers to a method of aiding individuals and systems to cope with these emotionally decisive moments in their lives. It includes pastoral counseling as well as other forms of pastoral care, and involves clergy as well as laypersons. It includes all helping activities designed to influence the course of a particular crisis so that those caught in its turmoil can return to their previous level of functioning and even achieve an enhanced ability to contend with future crises.

Ministers entering into an individual or family crisis have the dual objective of reducing the impact of the crisis-precipitating event and using the critical situation to help those affected strengthen their skills for solving future problems by learning more effective ways of coping. A crisis calls for new action, and its challenge has the potential to stimulate new ways of responding, increase capacity for living, and enhance mental and spiritual maturity. Crisis intervention is not just Band-Aid therapy—it is growth-oriented.

UNIQUE POSITION AND PERSPECTIVE

Clergy find themselves in a unique position for crisis intervention. For example, grief automatically brings the bereaved into the minister's compass. Pastors are often among the first to be sought out when crises arise, and are natural crisis interveners for a number of reasons.

First, clergy have a core of previously established relationships with people in the congregation. More than anyone else in the community, with the possible exception of the family doctor, they have cared for families during normal developmental crises and periods of stress. A pastor may have guided a family through some previous situational crisis, and therefore have specific knowledge not only of how the family handles stress but also intervention methods that were effective for them in the past.

Second, pastors have the advantage of immediacy; due to the clergy's availability and pastoral initiative, persons coming for help will not face weeks or even months of waiting lists, medical scrutiny, or the taking of long case histories. Unlike many other professionals, pastors can go where the people are. They are mobile—not tied to an office or bureaucratic red tape. They have always been able to make visits or schedule counseling appointments in places other than the office—traditionally in the home of the troubled persons. Visitation in hospital, workplace, and home helps pastors achieve a greater breadth of relationship. They come to know people in many more ways than the average psychiatrist or psychologist can know them; for example, carers in the church who observe that a family in serious crisis is not seeking help can seize the initiative, make pastoral visits, and offer assistance.

Third, clergy enjoy access to systems. Persons in crisis often are helped by the involvement of as many significant others as possible. Unlike many mental health professionals who have a strong individualistic focus, the clergy are oriented toward dealing with families and even extended families. Often they already know the family, friends, and relatives, and can call on them for assistance during the crisis.

Ministers doing crisis counseling are also unique in their ability to draw upon a support group from within the congregation. Therapists have no such source of committed individuals upon whom they can rely. Church members who volunteer to call or visit persons in distress offer not only assistance but a sense of belonging that can offset loneliness and isolation.

The community of faith is not only a specific geographical area, or a particular congregation of believers, but a common level of humanity that brings out the individual capacities of each person. It is not necessarily a place or a purpose, a size or a location, but the experience that one has in encountering others. The community of faith is constantly attuned to the Word of God in each individual situation. For example, the Word of God for a woman grieving the loss of her husband may mean no more than sitting with her; such a Word is not necessarily a verbal exercise. Where such community exists in a local congregation, persons in crisis are offered the support and caring of other members of the household of faith, the representative presence of the church.

Furthermore, to those in crisis, the very authority attributed to the pastor can serve the restoration of perspective and hope so desperately needed. "The person in crisis is one who has begun to lose perspective, feel anxious and helpless, often depressed and worthless, frequently without hope, whose future seems to be blocked out, who even has lost sight of some of his or her own past. Faith . . . is a direct counterforce to the dynamics of crisis" (Switzer 1986, 259).

Howard Clinebell (1984, 184) points out that "in crises and losses people often confront their spiritual hungers, the emptiness of their lives, and the poverty of their values and relationships." In the face of such emptiness, pastors—trained to deal with ultimate questions of meaning and value—can help people rediscover that living in relationship with a loving and faithful God provides meaning even in the midst of tragedy.

Thus *perspective* is a major difference between pastoral crisis intervention and crisis intervention offered by nonchurch mental health professionals. Ministers and mental health professionals may use many of the same intervention methods, but they approach them from different points of view. I have found that with people in crisis, questions concerning the meaning of suffering, life, death, and pain almost inevitably arise. No matter how troubled people depict their problems—mental, psychiatric, interpersonal, or intrapsychic—all crises are religious at their core, as Gerkin pointed out. They involve ultimate issues with which one must come to terms in the end.

Care and counseling offered by pastors is spiritual in its final and basic sense. LeRoy Aden (1968, 174) describes "final" in this regard as that which is ultimate from a long-term viewpoint, the end point of a process, whereas "basic" points to whatever is ultimate for humanity "in the present moment, to the depth dimension of a particular moment of time." Aden goes on to say that ministers' final and basic concerns differ from those of psychotherapists. Like all counselors, ministers must grapple with people's immediate problems; but "pastoral counseling has a different guiding image of man's plight and rescue, and therefore it often perceives in the client's verbalizations a different struggle and endpoint."

The pastor who witnesses the despair of a person who has suffered abuse and abandonment in childhood, endured years of hardship and failure, and now faces another emotionally hazardous situation, can convey the relevance of such theological concepts as theodicy (the goodness of God in the face of all the evil in the world), sacrifice, sin, grace, faith, and hope.

Many mental health professionals have recognized the importance of the spiritual dimension to those encountering problems of living. Carl Jung (1949, 264) wrote, "Among all my patients in the second half of life (that is to say, over thirty-five) there has not been one whose problem in the last resort was not that of finding a religious outlook on life." Eric Fromm (1947, 25) also recognized people's spiritual yearnings: "There is no one without a religious need, a need to have a frame of orientation and an object of devotion." Viktor Frankl (1963, 121), who spent three bleak years in a Nazi prison camp, strongly emphasized the need for meaning in life: "Woe to him who saw no more sense in his life, no aim, no purpose, and therefore no point in carrying on. He was soon lost."

Ministers unquestionably bring to people's crises distinct advantages and perspectives. Chief of these may be a relationship through which people in distress receive the clear sense that life has meaning, purpose, and hope.

TWO

The Dynamics of Crisis

> Meanwhile Saul, still breathing threats and murder against the disciples of the Lord, went to the high priest and asked him for letters to the synagogues at Damascus, so that if he found any who belonged to the Way, men or women, he might bring them bound to Jerusalem. Now as he was going along and approaching Damascus, suddenly a light from heaven flashed around him. He fell to the ground and heard a voice saying to him, "Saul, Saul, why do you persecute me?" He asked, "Who are you, Lord?" The reply came, "I am Jesus, whom you are persecuting. But get up and enter the city, and you will be told what you are to do." The men who were traveling with him stood speechless because they heard the voice but saw no one. Saul got up from the ground, and though his eyes were open, he could see nothing; so they led him by the hand and brought him into Damascus. For three days he was without sight, and neither ate nor drank. (Acts 9:1-9)

This passage from the New Testament is one of the most notable accounts of a sudden religious conversion—an event that can precipitate a crisis. Saul's experience was more remarkable than many conversions, resulting as it did from a dramatic vision. But in spite of—or even because of—these extreme circumstances, it illustrates how such an extraordinary experience can bring about a crisis in an individual's life.

Saul's dramatic conversion, occurring as he walked along the sun-baked Roman road outside Damascus, affected him physically—when he opened his eyes "he could see nothing" and had to be led by the hand into the city. The conversion also affected him mentally—he questioned his old beliefs and actions. Paul was changed spiritually as well—one of the most vigorous persecutors of Christianity became not only its ardent promoter but a theologian who wrote of the life of faith in clear and moving prose—who was persecuted for the faith. Finally, the conversion affected him emotionally—so much so that he abstained from food and drink for several days. Paul's conversion caused a crisis, a turning point, which affected every aspect of his life. He would never be the same—nor would the church.

A sound theoretical understanding is basic for effective ministry in a crisis. The purpose of this chapter is to describe the theory of crisis: how a crisis develops and the characteristics that mark its occurrence. Most people realize that crucial moments such as Paul experienced occur in their own lives, some becoming crises and others not. Because the methodology of crisis counseling works best for those who are actually in crisis, it is critical for helpers to examine what occurs in a situational crisis.

HOW A CRISIS DEVELOPS

A crisis occurs as an *internal* response to an *external* hazardous event. It is important not to confuse the crisis with the precipitating event. To this end it may be helpful to think of the development of a crisis in terms of four major elements (see diagram 1). The first is the stimulus or precipitating event. This is the external peril—such as death, divorce, or loss of a job—that theorists describe as an emotionally hazardous event.

DIAGRAM 1

Precipitating event → Appraisal → Resources and coping methods → Crisis

---

The second element of crisis development is the appraisal of the situation. It is what one makes of the precipitating event, one's perception of it as a hazard or threat. For a crisis to occur people must view the precipitator as a profound threat to their well-being or to the well-being of their family. They see it as a very dangerous situation, one that most likely will adversely affect their lives.

Everyone has a unique way of looking at a particular event. For example, one appraises the death of a close friend in terms of the past relationship with the deceased and one's previous experiences of loss; the appraisal also varies with the personality of each person affected. The immediacy of the loss, as well as its scope and impact for the bereaved, determines to a great extent whether a crisis will develop. Thus the widow of a twenty-six-year marriage who was deeply involved in the life of her husband will most likely perceive a greater loss than will the deceased's business acquaintances, whose relationships with him were limited to infrequent contacts. (Such a death could have a significant impact on the employees of the company he managed, however; they could appraise the death as a serious threat to their financial security and possibly go into crisis.)

The third factor leading to the development of a crisis is coping methods and personal resources. Coping methods are the manner in which people respond to problems; they are the strategies or steps one takes to resolve difficulties. Each person marshals external resources (such as friends, relatives, clergy, and physician) and internal resources (such as the ability to face and handle new situations, problem-solving, and communication skills) to meet the perceived threat. The adequacy of such resources and coping methods affects the extent to which an individual will experience the threat as a crisis.

Richard S. Lazarus (1966, 153) states that "when the individual discovers some important motive or value is being threatened, coping activity is mobilized by virtue of this threat, by virtue of the cognition that 'My life, health, wealth, or cherished social relationships are in danger.'" The goal of coping is the reduction or elimination of the appraised threat. If coping methods reduce the threat, a crisis is forestalled.

But if one's coping methods do not diminish the threat, a crisis will almost certainly occur. The *key* to the development of a crisis is that the person's appraisal process (perception) deems the precipitating event a serious threat, and the coping process does not readily ameliorate the threatening situation. Most theorists and practitioners agree that the resulting acute crisis usually lasts a maximum of six weeks, although the aftereffects of any crisis may continue for years. The crisis period of grief, for example, is only a short measure of the full skein of bereavement.

Thus a crisis is not an external event, although such an event is usually involved as a precipitator; a crisis is what happens within people, what takes place within families as a *response* to that event.

When all the employees of a small-town mine were laid off indefinitely after a protracted strike, they reacted differently because of their varying perceptions of the layoff and according to the diversity of their coping methods and resources. Michael Pulaski never cared much for his job, preferring to work as a handyman on evenings and weekends. He was saving money for his retirement, which he hoped would be no more than a few years off. When the union struck, Michael circulated cards advertising his home improvement services. His wife called people he had worked for in the past to see if they had other jobs for him or could refer him to others who might need things fixed in their homes. Michael had adequate financial resources, interpersonal relationships, and internal strengths, and he weathered the layoff with little or no experience of a crisis.

Other mine workers, like Allen Daniels, lacked Michael's resources, appraised the event as catastrophic, and went into a severe crisis. Allen experienced the layoff as an affront to his manhood. He become irritable and autocratic at home. He and his wife came to see me not because of the layoff at the mine, but because Mrs. Daniels was "fed up" with the way Allen was acting and she wanted a divorce. It took several counseling sessions to move them to an adaptive resolution of their situation. The two families clearly experienced the same precipitating event in disparate ways. For one it did not even cause a crisis, while for the other it shook the foundations of a twenty-year marriage.

CHARACTERISTICS OF CRISES

A useful way to understand what takes place in any given crisis is to consider the marks of a crisis. Crisis intervention theory asserts that, although the precipitators of crises vary greatly (death, infidelity, accident), all share particular patterns. This generic understanding of crisis allows ministers to care for people experiencing a wide range of troubling events, because some elements generally exist regardless of the precipitator. For the purposes of analysis, these characteristics will be separately listed, identified, and briefly discussed.

Previous Crises

Everyone has experienced a series of normal developmental crises in her or his life. Most have also experienced situational crises. In both cases they probably exhibited patterns of behavior that are common to all people in crisis.

The state of crisis had been assumed clinically but never demonstrated scientifically until crisis intervention theorist Howard Halpern set out to test the hypothesis that "crisis behavior would occur in individuals in crisis situations more significantly than in individuals in noncrisis situations" (1973, 344). Such behaviors included tiredness and exhaustion, helplessness, immobilization, confusion, physical symptoms, anxiety, disorganization of family relationships, and disorganization in social activities. He tested four typical groups of people whom one might expect to be in crisis: divorced persons, students seeking counsel at a mental health clinic, people in bereavement, and individuals entering mental hospitals. He compared them with a control group of persons who had not recently experienced any emotionally hazardous event. The testing and validation of this hypothesis may seem obvious and even unnecessary, but, as Halpern states, "Were this hypothesis not validated, the concept 'crisis' would be meaningless when applied to individuals because their behavior could not be differentiated from that of any individual selected from a noncrisis population."

Crisis behavior occurred significantly more often among people in the test group than among those in the control group. At the same time, Halpern's study found a lack of significant difference among the various types of crisis-precipitating events. No matter what precipitated the crisis, the pattern of response was very much the same. This similarity suggests a considerable commonality in the behavior of people who are in crisis, although what initiated it may be quite diverse. Thus studying and practicing crisis intervention techniques reduces the need to reinvent the wheel with each new precipitating event. Every crisis is unique in a number of respects; nevertheless, when someone in crisis comes to a minister, the minister can be reasonably sure that the person in crisis will exhibit a particular set of feelings and behaviors, and also has experienced them to some degree at an earlier time and place.

Crises as Normative

Crises are not a sign of mental illness but a normal human reaction to an emotionally hazardous situation. In physical disasters, such as floods or earthquakes, no one is surprised to see families or individuals with extreme emotional disturbance. Yet when the precipitator of the crisis is not physical but emotional or relational, such as bereavement or divorce, a stigma tends to be attached to resulting aberrations in behavior. In such situations the affected persons may even be labeled "mentally ill."

Frank Pittman, a family therapist, believes that when helpers encounter a family in crisis they "may find the family disorganized, non-functional, directionless, battling over long-dead issues" (1987, 4). He goes on to suggest that helpers may judge the family "far sicker than it is, assume the revived conflicts to be the real issues, and overlook the stress entirely." It is important to underscore that conflict and unhappiness are not necessarily synonymous with mental illness. In fact, in a bad situation, the existence of such conflict and unhappiness is more a sign of health than of illness. For example, a person who does not grieve the death of someone close is more to be suspected of emotional ill health than one who weeps for several weeks or even years afterward.

It must be noted, however, that although persons in crisis are not necessarily mentally ill, they may experience remarkably strong emotional reactions such as anxiety, depression, tension, panic, a personal and social sense of confusion and chaos, feelings of loss, helplessness, hopelessness, and disorganization. The emotional pain can lead to more serious distress if it is not resolved adaptively.

Crisis Precipitators

An outside precipitator or emotional hazard, such as death, divorce, or job loss, usually triggers a crisis; these precipitators are always situational and are frequently interpersonal in nature.

Halpern's study indicated no significant difference in the quality of the disturbance occasioned by the various precipitators. Nevertheless, some crisis precipitators (such as the death of a spouse) generally stimulate a greater degree of distress than others (such as the birth of a premature child). The extent and duration of the disturbance may be less in some of these secondary crises, but the quality of "being upset" will still manifest itself in a manner corresponding to cases of more severe crisis precipitators.

The precipitator of a crisis is usually one catastrophic event (like the death of a spouse), but it may also be the cumulation of a series of events. Individuals may weather a series of storms until one final event sends them crashing into the rocks. This final event may not seem like much of a precipitator to the helper (for example, a minor automobile accident with no physical injuries), but it is the proverbial straw that breaks the camel's back. People who apparently have coped well with a series of difficult events suddenly find themselves so exhausted that they cannot deal with one more problem. All their coping resources are spent and they are thrown into crisis.

Many writers who discuss the causes of emotional problems, such as those associated with divorce, tend to be overly simplistic. Clearly, not all divorced people experience the tumultuous feelings that these writers usually describe. Yet in crisis intervention this focus on the precipitator is critical. It is essential for both the minister and the crisis sufferer to identify the precipitating event.

In some situations, the precipitator is not readily recognizable to the person in distress. For example, a fifty-six-year-old man who went to his family doctor with stomach cramps and depression did not recognize any connection between the pain and his recent discovery that his son was a homosexual. Once the precipitator was uncovered, it became the object of the doctor's efforts to reduce the man's physical symptoms. "The crisis intervener is content . . . to deal primarily with precipitating causes. If someone is shaking with anxiety after an earthquake, one deals with the precipitant of the anxiety and is content to mollify or reduce the intensity of the symptom which resulted from the event" (Shneidman 1973, 10).

The Appraisal of a Threat

The precipitator and the crisis as such have no direct cause-and-effect relationship. In the face of an identical situation, one individual or family will appraise (perceive) it as emotionally hazardous and experience a crisis, while another will not look at it as an acute threat. When the aforementioned mine shut down, the Pulaskis responded quickly and well to the potential emotional hazard, and never experienced a crisis. The same event sent shock waves through the Daniels' household. One family carried on with equanimity, while the other family was nearly destroyed.

People's appraisals of emotionally hazardous situations, therefore, greatly determine whether a crisis will occur, and, if so, how serious it will become. Some precipitators have built within them an almost automatic crisis response. Heart attack, divorce, positive diagnosis of HIV, and death of a child or spouse are all precipitators that almost everyone sees as a serious threat.

For a crisis to develop, a serious threat to self or family has to be perceived—a threat grievous enough to cause disruption of what individuals value most. (I spoke of this factor in connection with the second of the four elements in the development of a crisis.)

During a crisis, people's mental circuits become overloaded. They see the threat as incompatible with their precrisis pattern of thinking about themselves or their world. This overload of incompatible information, sometimes called "cognitive dissonance," interferes with usual ways of planning and carrying out effective actions. The cognitive dissonance, which results from people's appraisal of the threat inherent in an event (learning that one has terminal cancer, for example), leads them first to try old and then new and different ways of eradicating the confusing feelings. Some individuals will respond adaptively and others will not. This is obvious to veterans of wartime experience; in a grisly battle some soldiers mature and become healthier mentally as a result of the experience; others fall apart, panic, desert, or break down. Few remain unaffected.

Crises and Loss

Most individuals in crisis perceive a loss or are threatened with the loss of something important to them—some source of physical, interpersonal, economical, or emotional well-being. The loss can be of a significant person, a love or dependency relationship, financial support, health, life, a familiar role, a sense of worthfulness, values, or meaning of life. Losses do not necessarily occur only in the form of divorce or death; significant loss can occur when an individual gets a new job or moves to a different part of the country.

When Bill was promoted from machinist to foreman, he gained greater prestige in the eyes of society, better pay, and greater job security. But he lost one of the things that was most important to him—his relationship with those who had been his colleagues (what Mitchell and Anderson [1983] call a role loss). Instead of talking and cracking jokes with his equals, he now had to prod subordinates to be more productive, and to report them if they were not. Bill found this role difficult; he was unhappy after his promotion and even talked of quitting. In handling such a loss, clergy who have confronted bereavement many times in their careers can confidently adapt and utilize the same methods with other losses not involving death.

Coping Methods and Resources

A crisis will occur only when early attempts at coping with the threat fail. ("Coping" refers to doing something—even if only choosing to accept one's lot—to resolve the perceived threat in the precipitator.) When habitual coping methods fail, disruption caused by the appraised threat remains or increases. People become immobilized or frantically continue trying those methods that have already proved inadequate for turning back the crisis. People in a crisis often say, "I just don't know what to do," or "I feel so helpless," or "I've tried everything and nothing seems to work." It is this paralysis that creates a crisis. Had they been able to use their regular coping methods and deal successfully with the perception of the event, they would not have experienced a crisis.

It is not unusual for people to have a number of misfortunes at once. They may have been handling several vexing situations with marginal effectiveness for a prolonged period of time, thus forestalling a crisis. When at last they reach a point of exhaustion, they lack strength to sustain their previously adequate coping resources, and everything falls apart. In such situations the stimulus for the crisis may appear minor to the helper; but a crisis is always of major importance to the person experiencing it, even if the precipitator seems insignificant to others.

The more seriously threatening one's appraisal of an event, the more primitive or regressive one's coping responses will be. Ministers often encounter persons in crisis who manifest considerable dependency and infantile clinging, which tend to repel others and provoke rejection and which can cause isolation.

The greater the number and diversity of coping methods, the more likely individuals will circumvent a crisis, or at least experience a milder crisis than those with poorer coping skills.

Heightened Psychological Accessibility

Heightened psychological accessibility is the most unique and important concept of crisis intervention theory. People in crisis are less defensive, more vulnerable, and more open to change than at other times in their lives. In families the boundaries are loosened, which helps ministers "or anyone else to enter and influence the way the system operates. Rules and roles become confused. Both expectations and prohibitions are relaxed" (Pittman 1987, 4). This heightened accessibility has obvious and important implications when it comes to helping a person in crisis. As Gerald Caplan, one of the early crisis intervention theorists, has stated, "A relatively minor force, acting for a relatively short time, can switch the whole balance to one side or the other—to the side of mental health or to the side of mental ill-health" (1964, 293). Thus a crisis can be a turning point in a person's emotional, mental, and spiritual health.

In his crisis research, Halpern validated Caplan's argument that people in crisis are more open to intervention of any kind, and he verified their heightened psychological accessibility. He found that those in crisis are less prone to protect themselves and are more open to outside help and assistance toward change.

The period of heightened psychological accessibility generally peaks quickly and lasts only briefly, usually a few days or weeks. Then a restoration of precrisis equilibrium occurs. (The restoration of equilibrium is not to be confused with the complete resolution of the problem that initially caused the crisis. For example, the heightened psychological accessibility of one who has been raped may last for only a week, but the scars of the abuse can remain for a lifetime.) When ministers do not establish a relationship quickly, spending too much time gathering information, persons in crisis will move beyond the point of heightened accessibility, and more time and effort will be required later than would have been necessary during the time of crisis.

One way to explain this period of heightened psychological accessibility is to use Morley's diagram of a crisis. In diagram 2 the triangle represents an individual who is not in crisis. This person is fairly stable;

DIAGRAM 2

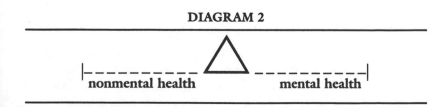

nonmental health   mental health

One of the sides of the triangle is firmly planted on a continuum between mental health and nonmental health. People are mostly stable and predictable when not in crisis and therefore are less open to change. A degree of stability is needed in order to live a normal life.

Diagram 3 illustrates a person who is in crisis, indicated by the triangle

DIAGRAM 3

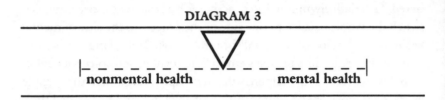

|⎯ ⎯|
nonmental health   mental health

that is tipped up on end. Here the person is in a state of being upset, or of cognitive dissonance. Much less of the personality is firmly planted on the line between mental health and nonmental health. The individual wants to reestablish stability and is therefore susceptible to any influence from the inside or outside that will aid in resolving the crisis. Thus with minimal effort, ministers, mental health professionals, or family members may exert a maximum amount of helping leverage on the individual.

I pointed out in *Suicide and Grief* (Stone 1972, 69–70) that "during the period of crisis, with individuals' greater susceptibility to change, less counseling is required to aid them toward effective resolution of their problems. The difficulty frequently is that we do not help soon enough. When the crisis stage is past, it takes more leverage to bring change because the 'triangle' is back on its base." The brief period when the triangle is tipped up is so significant because of the emotional intensity, the cognitive dissonance, the loosened boundaries, and the heightened vulnerability. Successful crisis intervention makes maximum use of the heightened psychological accessibility of individuals and families in crisis. All crisis counseling is based upon this principle.

Crisis as a Danger and Opportunity

Crisis resolution can be for better or for worse. Even though people may go through considerable emotional pain during a crisis, it can become a positive experience—a chance for growth. To let a crisis go by without learning from it is to waste a valuable opportunity.

Most ministers have seen both adaptive and unadaptive reactions among the bereaved. I recall Agatha, a thirty-seven-year-old woman in Los Angeles who stated that although she wished her husband had not died and would not like to go through the grief again, she felt she was a better person, more "alive," as a result of the experience. Before his death she was living in a rut, but since then she had increasingly valued her relationships with other people and with God. She had gained meaning in her life. She still grieved, yet she felt stronger than ever emotionally.

In sad contrast to Agatha is Horace, a fifty-seven-year-old man whom I counseled several times. Since his wife's death ten years ago he had lived under a cloud. He was chronically depressed and exhausted, and twice had entered a mental hospital, totally out of touch with reality. Horace thought about his late wife obsessively and kept several rooms of their home exactly as they were before she died. Unlike Agatha, who coped successfully with her crisis, Horace responded to the death of his wife in a most unadaptive way.

A history of successful resolution of past crises increases the chances of successfully resolving each new one. In the cases of Agatha and Horace, the vastly different reactions to bereavement were somewhat dependent upon how they dealt with previous crises in their lives. The cumulative effect of past unresolved problems can combine with new crises to make them even harder to resolve. Agatha had weathered a number of earlier, less serious crises, and they better prepared her to cope with what is for most people the worst crisis precipitator they will face. Horace had a history of adapting poorly to stressful situations, especially to the death of his mother. In his case the triangle tipped toward danger, while for Agatha it became an opportunity.

Crises of Religious Values

Paul Tillich defined pastoral care as a "helping encounter in the dimension of ultimate concern" (quoted in Clinebell 1984, 67). Besides causing upheaval in an individual's emotional, physical, and intellectual life, a crisis also can upset a person's values and sense of meaning. One encounters the basic contradiction between infinite aspirations and finite possibilities (Gerkin 1979). Every crisis raises at its core issues of faith, and asks questions such as: What is the meaning of life? Is it worth the pain to continue living? Did I do the right thing? Why did this happen to me? Why does God allow me to suffer? Can I ever trust anyone again? Asking these questions requires an openness to the vulnerability of an unknowable future; they require the making of faith choices. "Hope that is seen is not hope. For who hopes for what is seen? But if we hope for what we do not see, we wait for it with patience" (Rom. 8:24-25).

Ministers or counselors who deal with the emotional, physical, or intellectual life and ignore the spiritual core of crises are not responding to the whole person. During crises, because of their heightened psychological accessibility, people may be especially receptive to issues of faith if they are sensitively portrayed.

Conversely, during a crisis, upstanding members of a congregation may question in their faith what they had previously affirmed. The minister needs to remain emotionally with them at such times. The helper's sensitivity and ministry of presence can aid them in weathering their uncertainty (Stone 1988).

Crises Ministry as the Priesthood of All Believers

Intervention in crises is not the exclusive domain of clergy and mental health professionals. The entire priesthood of believers is called to a ministry of caring for the neighbor. The empathy, warmth, and concern of laypersons and significant others may be both necessary and sufficient in the resolution of a crisis. Pastors are not offering optimal care when, hearing of a crisis, they don their white hat, mount their steed, and charge to the rescue—ignoring the considerable assistance lay ministers have to offer. Effective crisis intervention counseling by clergy may often involve little more than enabling others to care for those in crisis.

People's Expectations

All persons who come for help come with a particular set of expectations, the fulfillment of which is one of the most important factors in arriving at a positive outcome. In some forms of traditional counseling, psychotherapists endeavor to go beneath the original problem and expectations of clients to the deeper underlying ones. This approach may be valuable in long-term therapy, but in crisis intervention it is important to work, wherever possible, toward the fulfillment of people's stated goals. The minister's task is to assist them in discerning exactly what they expect to achieve (the goal) and then to help them reach it.

Changing the Situation

Situational aspects frequently are factors in sustaining a crisis; altering the environment often can change the course of a crisis positively.

Alicia Brown, a twenty-nine-year-old Philadelphian whose husband had abandoned her five weeks before she sought help, was the mother of four children from two to eight years old. Alicia's crisis was precipitated when the utility companies turned off her electricity and gas in the middle of winter, and the landlord gave her two days to come up with the back rent or be put out in the street.

She tried in vain for one whole day to borrow the money she needed. Finally she walked into a downtown church and told the minister her situation. Within twenty-four hours the minister was able to find Alicia another apartment, arrange for several church members to help her move, and put her in touch with a social worker who would help her obtain money and food for herself and her children.

The alteration of her environmental situation—moving to another apartment and receiving some money and food—resolved her immediate crisis. She had other problems, but changing these basic situational obstacles in the life of her family moved Alicia to a place where she could start addressing her other difficulties one at a time. The immensity of the immediate problem had paralyzed her so that she was not able to do anything—even basic things like feeding her children.

Need for Positive Relationships

People in crisis often tend to pull away from the very interpersonal relationships that they need more than ever—whether out of embarrassment, an instinct to be alone and lick one's wounds, confusion about what to do, or a desire to hide the crisis from others. Positive interpersonal relationships foster adaptive crisis resolution.

A significant factor in the resolution of Alicia's crisis was her willingness to seek help from others. A troubled person is not an isolated individual, but an interacting member of a social system. In crisis intervention the minister needs to realize that, for instance, if a woman has lost her job, the crisis may involve not only her but her husband and children as well. Persons in crisis need other caring people around them. (In this regard, couples in the process of divorce are particularly needy because they are frequently treated as emotional lepers at a time when they require friends and relatives more than ever.) A lack of valuable interpersonal relationships will almost certainly heighten the suffering of persons in crisis.

Equipped with a basic understanding of the dynamics and characteristics of crisis, ministers can begin to utilize these insights to ease the distress of people coming to them for help. They can view the singularity of each individual human situation in balance with the knowledge of experiences common to all who find themselves in crises, facilitating an orderly and tested approach to the resolution of these boundary experiences.

THREE

A Design for Intervention

Hector Mercado called his pastor at 11:45 P.M. Thursday night. He and his wife had fought again, and she wanted a divorce. Pastor Cole knew that Hector, twenty-nine, and Donna, twenty-seven, had been having trouble for the six years they had been married, though whenever he visited them in their home they always acted the happily married couple. Hector did not want a divorce.

Hector asked Pastor Cole to come immediately, but the pastor, determining that there was no immediate physical danger, set up an appointment for the next morning at his office. When they arrived late Donna stated, "I only came because he wanted me to. I've made up my mind: I'm going to get a divorce and neither you nor anybody else can change my mind." She felt their relationship was beyond help.

Hector said the problem was that she wanted a divorce. Donna said the problem was Hector and everything he did. Pastor Cole arranged to see the couple again three days later. He telephoned their home several times between sessions without reaching either of them.

At the appointed hour Hector showed up alone. He said that Donna had forced him out of the house and he was staying at his brother's place. He cried through most of the session. All he could think about was the tremendous loss he had sustained, and all he wanted out of counseling was to get back his wife. "There is nothing left in life anymore without her," Hector said. "If she doesn't come back I'm going to kill myself."

How might this situation be handled? What would be the best approach in dealing with Hector Mercado?

These questions deserve an immediate answer, as surely as Hector needed immediate help. Before dealing with them, however, it would be useful to consider more fully a design for pastoral crisis intervention. The crisis intervention methods described in this chapter are designed to take full advantage of the healing and growth-fostering forces that already exist in individuals such as Hector (especially those in crisis who seem to be without them) and of the distinctive opportunities for caring inherent within the church.

ADVANTAGES OF CRISIS INTERVENTION METHODS

Crisis intervention methods have several advantages over traditional counseling practice in times of a crisis such as the one Hector Mercado experienced. First, crisis intervention methods are designed specifically to deal with crisis, not with other problems. Just as some methods are especially effective with autistic children, and others with chronic depressive individuals, crisis intervention methods have been designed to take advantage of the unique aspects of a crisis and to use the heightened psychological accessibility to its full benefit.

Second, clergy sometimes encounter backlash from people with whom they have had long-term, in-depth counseling relationships. Because crisis intervention is short-term in nature and focuses on immediate problem solving, parishioners need not fear that the minister will delve into all the dark nooks and crannies of their psyches; they are less likely to resent their pastor or leave the church later, out of embarrassment. (It can still happen!)

Third, crisis intervention is effective with individuals from a wide range of cultural and socioeconomic groups. According to Gerald Jacobson (1965, 214–15), any helping that finds the helper and the one seeking help "psychosocial strangers must, at least at first, minimize the differences between the persons involved and maximize what unites them. . . . The more acute the crisis, the less the sense of strangeness, even with patients and therapists widely divergent in social background or age." Especially among poorer people, a demand for immediate and concrete action rather than delaying gratification for the sake of long-term mental health goals is common. Crisis intervention is geared to this need.

Fourth, as a brief method of pastoral care and counseling, crisis intervention does not use up large periods of the pastor's time. Because a crisis' duration is at most six weeks, the minister will not face a long-term time commitment.

Finally, crisis intervention is a method of pastoral care that not only pastors but also trained laypersons in the congregation can practice. It is most effective with training and supervised practice; although to be a competent crisis intervener, years of training in psychodynamics, pathology, and analysis are unnecessary.

PREPARING TO COUNSEL DURING CRISES

Ministers need to prepare themselves on a number of levels to deal with crucial situations. One area they cannot overlook is their own personal issues that may rise to the surface when they encounter crisis situations. The following are some personal preparations I have found valuable.

First, I have to reflect on the care that I offer and the motives behind my helping acts—to recognize that at times I get in the way of my caring for others. If a person's crisis is similar to one I experienced recently or never completely resolved, my ability to help may be impaired, and at such times I need help. Help can take the form of case consultation, or referral, which I discuss at the end of this chapter. I need to know my own limitations in order to function effectively as a pastoral carer.

Second, I have to prepare to accept failure. Definitions of success and failure are elusive, but I know that sometimes, no matter how hard I try to rationalize, I feel as if I have failed. True, I have made mistakes; but also true is that people often resist help when they seriously need it. Some people would commit suicide rather than share their deepest feelings. Because all change is experienced as loss, people in crisis will naturally have mixed feelings about making changes. This ambivalence may affect the outcome of any attempt at intervention.

Third, I have to be sensitive to expectations others have of me as a pastor, and to the role they assign me—perhaps a reflection of their childhood experiences with a minister. Most people do not know how to act in counseling. Their impressions largely reflect stereotypes from literature, media, even comic strips. I can still see the startled look on the face of a late-middle-aged woman who first saw a youngish-looking pastoral counselor without a tie or coat and exclaimed, "You're not *Doctor* Stone, are you?!" (The woman later explained that she had expected me to be fifty, gray, and bearded. Some twenty years later, I seem to have fulfilled her stereotypes.) One impression is the notion that ministers and counselors can wave a magic wand and solve any problem. The magic may occasionally work in the helper's favor—but never for long.

Fourth, I also need to prepare for pastoral crisis intervention by conditioning and improving my ability to cope with negative feelings— anger, sarcasm, and belittlement—directed toward me. During my freshman year in college I was canvassing for a local inner city church in Minneapolis. We were instructed to ask a few basic questions and then be ready to sit and talk with anyone who requested it. At one apartment I encountered a man in his forties who gruffly invited me in. After I had settled myself and asked five or six questions about his church affiliation, he said, "You're a Christian—I have a question for you. My son was killed—run over by a car two weeks ago. Why did God do that? Why did God allow it to happen?" He proceeded to berate me about the hypocrisy of Christians, the foolishness of religion, and the fact that I had no answers to his questions. I agonized through his angry words and gesticulations, frozen to my chair with fear. If he had not been between me and the door I would have fled. After what seemed like hours but was probably minutes, he broke down and cried, "You're the first one who has listened to me." Although I take no credit for the way I handled the situation—I listened because I could not find a way out—I was able to give him the chance he needed to release some feelings about his son's death.

Sometimes we have to wade through the murky waters of black and angry emotions to be able to care for someone. I am not suggesting that caregivers become emotional whipping posts, but in crises people sometimes share things that they later regret. Helpers can expect to stay up late many evenings, miss an occasional day off, and give generously of themselves—only to receive either no thanks or even hostility from the recipient of their care.

Another danger I must prepare for is the possibility of going into a crisis myself while caring for others. When this happens the helper loses the ability to relate in a calm and relaxed manner, and to see alternative solutions to a problem. Ministers react differently to the anxiety of a crisis—some talk too much or fail to listen closely, others quote Scripture or give authoritarian dictates, and still others become paralyzed. Whatever response anxiety produces, be aware of it and develop ways to circumvent it. The best course when sensing the personal onset of a crisis-like state is to share the burden with someone else—a minister or mental health worker—by inviting a capable helper to share the responsibility for the case (essential when a person is suicidal) or by referring those for whom you are caring to another source of help. I always have found that by sharing a troubling situation with at least one other person I give myself a chance to release my own anxieties and allow myself to get another perspective on the crisis.

One prerequisite for crisis counseling is necessary for all pastoral care work: to care genuinely for the person in crisis. If one becomes so concerned with one's role, intervention techniques, or with other personal responsibilities that one loses sight of the mission to love others, then a caregiver can miss seeing a person in crisis as infinitely worthful. This aspect of preparation may seem so obvious that it need not be mentioned, yet at times parishioners or counselees can become cases, problems, or new experiences rather than unique and precious human beings.

THE A-B-C METHOD OF CRISIS INTERVENTION

The goal of crisis counseling is to help persons in crisis regain at least their precrisis level of functioning, and (one hopes) to grow to even higher levels. The first step toward this goal is to determine if a crisis really exists. Switzer (1986, 41) believes that this can be ascertained by answering three questions: "(1) Has there been a recent (within a few weeks) onset of the troublesome feelings and/or behavior? (2) Have they tended to grow progressively worse? (3) Can the time of onset be linked with some external event, some change in the person's life situation?" If the answer to all three questions is yes, then a crisis most likely exists.

The model of crisis intervention offered here is my adaptation of the ABC method first formulated by psychiatrist Warren L. Jones (1968, 87), as a technique of helping people in crisis. (His method was further developed and confirmed by Howard Clinebell and David Switzer as well as such theorists as Robert Carkhuff, Allen Ivey, and William Glasser.)

The A-B-C method of pastoral crisis intervention has three elements: (A) Achieve contact with the person; (B) Boil down the problem to its essentials; and (C) Cope actively with the problem. This method does not require a progression from A to B to C. Two or three steps can and frequently do occur at the same time.

Achieving Contact with the Person in Crisis

The initial step for helping individuals in crisis is to achieve contact—to establish an empathetic relationship. If a relationship already exists, it can speed the initial phase of crisis intervention. A solid supportive relationship not only serves to help troubled people to feel comfortable but also becomes the means through which the minister can move them from catharsis (the release of emotions) to action. The relationship is not the goal of crisis intervention but the basis upon which the care process grows toward crisis resolution.

A relationship of trust and empathy is no less important in crisis intervention than in any other form of counseling or pastoral care, but because persons in crisis are usually less defensive, less time and effort is usually required to establish it. In establishing relationships, crisis intervention helpers use basic relation-building skills: attending behaviors and listening.

Attending Behaviors. Attending behaviors are the minister's physical, nonverbal acts that communicate interest and concern and help produce a relaxed and comfortable environment for people. They are a way of saying "I care about you." A variety of behaviors serve this function.

One attending behavior valuable in the development of a relationship is symbolic nourishing. Perhaps the first way we experience the care of another is nursing at our mother's breast or being held and fed by either parent. Indeed, from infancy, one of the simplest and most effective ways in which we preceive the concern and care of others is through actual and symbolic nourishment with food and drink. Delivering a coffee cake or a cooked meal to a bereaved family is an example of this attending behavior. Also, providing a comfortable, relaxed environment and a cup of coffee or a glass of water shows concern.

Physical posture, sometimes referred to as "body language," also can communicate interest and readiness to respond. The most helpful posture is to face people and lean forward slightly. Consider your own response: When you are deeply interested in what someone is saying, you often move to the edge of your chair to hear better. Such a move closes the physical distance and signals active interest.

Another way we experience care and concern from earliest infancy is by being held and cuddled by our parents. The need for touch continues into adulthood. Holding the hand of a person in grief, putting an arm around the shoulder of one who is upset, even a handshake, are ways of gently communicating concern through touch. The great benefit of touch is that it can transmit feelings of concern when words are impossible; most pastors have experienced these moments of contact at the bedside of someone who is dying. Caution: Behavior that is appropriate in public—hugging after worship, for example—is likely inappropriate in an ongoing, caregiving situation. All attending behaviors, especially touching, must be offered only when they will assist the person; some people object to being touched. In addition, in crisis intervention, a person of the opposite gender may interpret touching as a sexual gesture.

Looking into the eyes of a troubled person is one of the most powerful attending behaviors for communicating concern. Some people cannot verbalize without this eye contact. One day, when I was talking with a professor in her classroom, she turned away to wipe off the blackboard; as she did so I stopped talking without noticing it. She turned back to me and remarked, "You need eye contact, don't you?" She realized the importance of eye contact, recognizing that the amount of eye contact required varies from individual to individual. If persons are given too much eye contact, they will show their discomfort, visibly looking away or pulling back in their chair or closing their eyes. Some, of course, will share their discomfort verbally. However, if the amount of eye contact is too brief, they may be reluctant to share their problems and feelings in more than a superficial manner.

The room in which the caregiver receives a person needs to communicate calmness, confidentiality, and openness. Ideally, both the caregiver and the person seeking help should be sitting in comfortable chairs of equal height, facing each other. Doors to the room should be shut and noises from the outside not allowed to intrude, so that the person has confidence that no one can overhear the conversation. If the room is reasonably in order, and the temperature and lighting are at comfortable levels, the individual will relax more.

The environment will not always be ideal; care can be offered in a kitchen, walking down a street, or standing in an emergency ward. Nevertheless, the most relaxed area that is conducive to private conversation should be sought. Move from the kitchen to a living room or den; leave the street for a quiet coffee shop; step out of the hospital waiting room and into the respite offered by the chapel. The setting at which listening occurs can greatly affect the troubled person's openness to attempts at caring.

Listening. The second important skill in establishing a relationship is listening, which in some respects might be considered an attending behavior. Giving full and undivided attention to what persons in crisis are saying communicates caring and concern. To quote Dietrich Bonhoeffer (1954, 97):

> The first service that one owes to others in the fellowship consists in listening to them. Just as love of God begins with listening to His Word, so the beginning of love for [others] is learning to listen to them. It is God's love for us that He not only gives us His Word but also lends us His ear. So it is His work that we do for [others] when we learn to listen to them. Christians, especially ministers, so often think they must always contribute something when they are in the company of others, that this is the one service they have to render. They forget that listening can be a greater service than speaking.

Bonhoeffer captured an important attitude of the Christian life: *listening*—to God and to neighbor. The following are some suggestions for responsive listening, which is vital in crisis intervention.

Outside distractions, such as noise or phone calls, can interrupt persons who are attempting to reveal something important. Of course, these distractions should be avoided or minimized. But inner distractions, such as thinking about all the other things yet to be done in the day, can also impede listening. People usually sense such inner distance and avoid revealing much about themselves.

Inappropriate attending behaviors—chuckling as the other person approaches tears—can also divert a person's self-disclosure. When the listener's behaviors are not congruent with the feelings being expressed, the person may perceive that she or he is being mocked and, as a result, may talk less freely. As with Saint Paul, "Rejoice with those who rejoice, weep with those who weep" (Rom. 12:15).

The listening needs to focus on the presenting problem and the precipitator of the crisis. How does the person in crisis perceive the emotionally hazardous situation? What coping methods and resources have been used to deal with the crisis? Sensing how this person experiences the stress of the crisis is important because in step B, the boiling down process, the person needs help in focusing on what the crisis means to him or her personally.

Temporarily suspending all judgments allows the individual to release pent-up emotions. Especially in the early phases of a relationship, criticism—or evaluations that are taken as such—can make the person reticent to continue sharing; many will shut down altogether in the face of perceived judgment. Judgment may sometimes be needed in pastoral care, but not until a solid relationship is established and usually not when the person is in a crisis state.

Individuals in crisis sometimes have difficulty saying clearly what they want to express, and helpers need to be patient. In the confusion of a crisis, people's mental processes are not functioning normally; they may experience pain which is so deep that they have difficulty verbalizing it. For example, how can the depth of pain felt immediately after the death of someone close be expressed in words? At first it is valuable to allow long pauses before responding to what is said. Most beginning crisis interveners are overly anxious about filling in these silences; as a result, instead of listening, they are busy figuring out what to say next.

Ministers need to attend to important themes as a person speaks about the crisis. Such themes can be recognized because they are usually stated repeatedly or with great intensity. These recurring themes will be valuable clues in helping people to focus on the essence of their distress.

In crisis intervention, unlike some methods of helping, it is important early on to let people know that time is of the essence. Narrowing the focus of communication, by selectively reinforcing those subjects that are related to the crisis and by withholding response to those that are irrelevant, is the key. It is best to allow people considerable freedom in the first one-third to one-half of the initial interview, but thereafter to focus the conversation on the actual crisis. Often, it is enough to say,

"That sounds like something important that we should deal with, but it doesn't seem directly related to your present problem. As soon as we have somewhat resolved this crisis we can return to it."

Without realizing it, ministers may in their counseling encourage a return to ineffective childhood behaviors: by allowing rambling or unfocused conversation or talk that mainly focuses on past events; by not encouraging people to use their own resources of self-observation, self-restraint, and self-responsibility; by allowing them to detach from their feelings without calling them back to awareness; or by permitting anything to keep them from focusing on the immediate crisis.

Psychotherapists are trained to avoid taking too much responsibility in counseling, but the crisis helper sometimes needs to be active and assertive (even breaking confidentiality in rare but necessary cases such as threatened violence) in order to make decisions for those who are unable to handle the decision-making process on their own. Such persons need a crisis intervener who does more than reflect feelings or offer passive support. In other words, it is the caregivers' task to take responsibility, but only to the extent it is needed. As Thomas Rusk (1971, 251) puts it, "Do for others that which they cannot do for themselves, and no more."

While establishing the relationship, caregivers should communicate as much as possible their own self-confidence, stability, and willingness to take an active role. A troubled individual, particularly in crisis, initially may be unable to act or decide or take any responsibility alone, and needs to sense these strengths within the pastoral carer. Attending and listening communicates a genuine love and a depth of involvement and caring.

Boiling Down the Problem to Its Essentials

The second step of the A-B-C method of crisis intervention involves reducing the problem to its essential elements. This step requires responding to people in crisis in such a way that they can define in their own minds what has happened, what they are feeling, and why. The boiling down phase calls upon the helper's skills of responding and focusing.

Responding. Responding is one of the basic dimensions of all human interchange; communication, verbal or nonverbal, is not complete until there is response. Helpers have already begun responding to persons in crisis while achieving contact (A), but during the boiling down phase (B) helpers will have fewer and shorter periods of only listening.

To go beyond attending and listening and to begin boiling down the problem to its essentials, it is necessary to distinguish between facilitative and nonfacilitative ways of responding. The following are *not* helpful ways of responding to those in crisis.

One of the quickest ways to miss the pain of others and to leave them feeling unheard is to offer *quick advice*. For example, making suggestions only ten minutes after a person starts talking does not take seriously what the other has to say or the complexity of the issues involved. Furthermore, advice offered before a solid relationship has been established will probably go unheeded. Only after a caring relationship has been founded and alternative strategies of action have been explored can tentative offerings of advice be helpful.

Likewise, *false assurances* accomplish nothing. Telling a wife whose husband has just left her, "I'm sure he'll come back," or a person facing exploratory surgery, "Everything is going to be just fine," assumes a knowledge you do not possess. Most people reject such statements as insincere—they may even mumble, "How do you know?" It is desirable to support an individual emotionally and to reassure him or her realistically; it is inauthentic and inappropriate to promise what is impossible to predict.

Well-meaning but ineffectual helpers sometimes summarize complex problems in the form of *bromides,* such as "God helps those who help themselves"; "If you make your bed, you have to lie in it"; "A fellow ought to go out and sow some wild oats before he settles down." Bromides contain some kernels of truth but are not very personal or helpful. Responses ought to be specific, clear, and individually tailored to the issues about which the troubled person is talking. The greater the specificity of a response, the greater the applicability of the help offered.

The number of *questions* posed to people in crisis should be kept to a minimum because questions tend to put people on the spot and narrow their range of expression. Closed-ended queries such as "How old are you?" "Did you want to marry him in the first place?" "How many years did you go together?" "Did you love her?" call only for a word or a phrase reply and do not allow others to tell their own stories in their own ways. Open-ended questions are more effective: "How have you felt recently about your husband?" "What are your concerns about this operation?" "What is it like at home now that your last daughter has moved out?" "Tell me about . . ."

Judgmental pronouncements, such as "That's dumb"; "You were foolish to tell your husband about your affair"; or "A Christian should not smoke," are apt to do more harm than good. God's love is meted out in both judgment and grace, and sometimes it is difficult for Christians to remain morally neutral; but in a helping relationship passing judgment ignores the complexities of the troubled person's problems. After a relationship is well established and considerable listening has occurred, it may be appropriate to voice a personal understanding of the ethics of a given situation—as long as this statement remains tentative and gentle, allowing the other to sense the compassion and hear the concern that prompts such a witness.

Psychoanalysis is best left to therapists' offices and cocktail parties, and responses should be made directly to what has been said. Statements like "That's probably because of the harsh treatment your mother gave you" or "You're doing that because of your resentment toward women" are examples of interpretive responses and are not helpful. The minister should let each individual draw his or her own conclusions.

Debating or arguing with a person who is experiencing a crisis usually creates distance rather than closeness. The caregiver needs to respect the right of persons to maintain their own, different views by neither criticizing nor belittling those persons or their views.

Finally, although sharing personal struggles and joys as one finite human being with another can be effective, using the relationship as a place to *seek release* is not proper. The caregiver should get help, if needed, from others.

Probably the best way to develop effective, facilitative responding skills is to learn mirroring, or reflecting back in a sentence or two the essence of what the other person has shared ("I hear you saying you feel . . ."). In establishing a relationship it is best to respond at first primarily to feelings. As the relationship develops, both feelings and content become increasingly important because the two together reveal the meaning of what is being expressed. For example: "I hear you saying you feel low" reflects a feeling (depression), whereas "because you lost your job" reflects content (being fired). Only when the two are viewed together is the full meaning apparent. The cause of the depression is recognized when the content is added—the loss of the job. The following are additional features of effective response and good feedback.

• *Specificity*. Vague or general responses, such as "You are too aggressive," are hard for the person to use. "You speak loudly and interrupt others frequently" is more helpful feedback, describing behaviors that a person can observe and alter.

• *Using open-ended questions*. Ask as few questions as possible and make them open-ended, requiring more than a simple yes or no.

• *Describing rather than evaluating*. Describing a feeling response to something the person has said is better than putting a label on that statement: "I sense you have reservations about making these changes" rather than "you're stubborn."

• *Responding with immediacy*. It is important to give frequent feedback, at the appropriate time, rather than save it all up for a summarizing conclusion.

• *Brevity*. Limiting most responses to a sentence or two whenever possible is better than lengthy responses.

• *Checking for understanding*. If any uncertainty remains regarding understanding—whether you have understood or been understood correctly—inquire about this. One way to check is to have the other rephrase what he or she heard (that is, mirror back to the caregiver).

• *Pauses*. It is better to allow lapses in conversation when they occur naturally and not to pepper the dialogue with new questions whenever the person takes a breath. Pauses not only allow the individual to reflect on what has been said but also give the carer a chance to formulate responses without using valuable listening time to do so.

Focusing. Individuals are frequently not fully aware of the precipitating stress and its consequences. The focusing process aims at prompt identification of the nature of the threat, and clarification of the relevant circumstances and conflicts. When the crisis can be defined clearly and the nature of the threat to the person clarified, a plan for its resolution becomes possible; indeed, ideally it would emerge out of the individual's own thinking.

Many in crisis are momentarily evading reality and defending themselves against pain, thus part of the helper's task is to encourage them to face up to reality. The caregiver creates an environment in which the person feels comfortable enough to confront the crisis and the event that precipitated it. In focusing, the minister needs to be aware of the following: (1) the precipitating event; (2) the loss or threatened loss of something or someone important; (3) the individual's coping methods and resources; and (4) new factors or conditions which may cause his or her traditional methods of coping to fail.

Focusing includes filtering out irrelevant data. Persons in crisis sometimes share material that is meaningless to the situation that they do not know is meaningless. If a person brings up seemingly unrelated material, the minister can try to relate it to the present crisis—or show its irrelevance—with a statement such as, "I wonder how you see this relating to your immediate problem."

Once the situation is accurately assessed, the minister communicates the essence of the dilemma as simply and directly as possible. This communication has been called "consensual formulation." The minister and the individual mutually formulate an understanding of what has happened and put it into words. The distressed person is able to move to the next elements of the crisis intervention process: examining alternative methods of dealing with the present crisis, choosing those which seem appropriate, and mobilizing available resources. When consensual formulation is not developed (and it may not always be possible), there is less chance for personal growth and learning from the crisis, even though the crisis may be resolved adaptively.

The development of a consensual formulation can in itself reduce the anxiety level and enhance the self-esteem of the person in crisis. It accomplishes a basic purpose of crisis counseling, namely, to help the person pull out of the tailspin.

Coping Actively with the Problem

In the final stage of the A-B-C method, ministers help those in crisis evaluate and mobilize their resources, develop a plan of action, and make specific changes directed toward resolving the crisis. The ultimate goal of all helping is *action*—such as making a decision, accepting a loss that cannot be changed, learning a new skill, or finding a job. Thoughtful yet decisive action leads to growth.

Knowing what the problem is but being unable to find a solution is a common difficulty for those in crisis, yet it is useless to boil down the problem if the person does not take action. Each pastoral carer requires a systematic model or models in order to help people weigh alternatives, make decisions, and take the first steps toward problem resolution. Problem management methods are based on the assumption that merely communicating about a problem and expressing one's feelings about it are not always sufficient. In some cases the problem persists (for example, the alcoholic husband who continues beating his wife whenever he drinks) until the person takes action and begins to make responsible choices.

The minister needs to help those in crisis examine alternative courses of action with which they can take to reshape their lives, and then needs to challenge them to act upon one or more of those alternatives. Such problem management usually has five components: establishing goals; taking inventory of resources; formulating alternatives; committing to action; and evaluating.

Establishing Goals. Ideally, at this point in the A-B-C method, the minister has established a relationship, allowed the expression of feelings, and helped the person boil down and define the problem. The next task is to establish goals. This task is usually fairly simple, inasmuch as crisis counseling aims only at the removal of symptoms and the achievement of a level of functioning as high as or higher than before.

Changing the focus of helping from negative (problems) to positive (goals) is the first step. Once some general, long-term goals are stated, it is important to develop specific, short-term, easily attained objectives toward which the problem solving will be aimed. For example, if the problem is that a void was created when a couple's last daughter joined the Air Force and moved to another country, the goal is to find new tasks and meaning now that the nest is empty and only long-distance parenting is required; one objective may be to start up the mail-order business they had talked about for years but never seemed to have time to put into operation.

The goal determines the direction in which the care will proceed and toward which the courses of action will be aimed. It is always best to be as specific as possible in defining goals, and to express them in observable terms. It is far more helpful to establish small and short-term aims, and attain them, than to set up lofty, long-term goals that may not be reached and will bring disappointment. Most of the useful goals in crisis counseling should be attainable in a matter of weeks.

Taking Inventory of Resources. After the goal has been delineated, ministers will need to help individuals take inventory of their internal and external resources. People in crisis sometimes have trouble reviewing their resources rationally, and the minister may have to take the lead.

Internal resources are those methods of coping which each person has developed and upon which he or she can draw in the face of daily problems. Sometimes people are not aware of their internal resources. The minister needs to point them out by saying, for example: "You say you can't tell people what you feel, but I see you doing a great job of telling your feelings to me." One significant internal resource is the experience of handling past crises. Once again, the minister who previously has shared developmental or situational crises with people is in a good position to help them discover what led to their successful resolution and apply those lessons to their present troubles.

External resources include friends, family, church, community groups, and finances. People who are in crisis often pull away from meaningful interpersonal involvement and feel lonely. A relatively modest degree of concern on the part of others often is enough to exert a great deal of positive influence upon those in crisis. The support that a now-lost relationship had offered may be regained through contact with a new significant person or through the strengthening of a pre-existing relationship.

Those who are emotionally close to a person in crisis frequently need pastoral care as well. They are under greater-than-normal pressures during the crisis and may themselves require special guidance and support, though not necessarily from the minister. Here an organized program of lay pastoral care, involving people in the congregation who are capable and willing to move into crisis situations and are not frightened by them, can be of great help (Stone 1991).

Individuals in crisis can find additional support in ongoing fellowship or prayer groups within the church. The worship and occasional services of the church (a funeral service, confession, or an order for the Blessing of a Civil Marriage) may also offer an important resource in a crisis.

Even in the most remote rural area, community resources are probably available in times of crisis. They include counseling agencies, visiting nurses, adult day care, treatment centers, support groups, local business and service organizations and a host of other supportive activities. Even ordinary people may be marshalled to lend a hand, raise money, give blood, sit with the bereaved. Individuals who have recently been in counseling are best referred back to the same counselor (one should carefully evaluate protests such as "she didn't help me" before accepting them at face value). People in crisis also may resist listing as resources those whom they feel are unwilling or unable to help. Others often become irritated by the whining, dependency, depression, and help-lessness that crises sometimes bring out in people, but they are more likely to mobilize if the minister can make them see the extent of the need and their potential for offering support. Therefore one task in crisis intervention is to help these significant others care for the troubled person as effectively as possible.

Formulating Alternatives. After developing goals and reviewing re-sources, the minister and the persons in crisis brainstorm alternative courses of action that might facilitate these goals. The minister en-courages individuals to develop their own alternatives, and both good and bad ideas are included on the list of ideas (for example, a suicidal individual includes committing suicide as an option). The caregiver can jar their thinking by suggesting courses of action they would never have considered. This is not a matter of advice-giving but an attempt to broaden the horizons of persons who may still be cognitively constricted and who cannot think of alternatives; in almost every case, the individual personally chooses the course of action to take.

From the list of alternatives the minister and the person in crisis weed out all irrelevant and unworkable courses of action. For example, the single mother who feels pressured by the responsibilities of home, three children, and a full-time job may not be able to quit her job and stay home. If she has no other means of income, such a course would be impossible even if it were desirable. The person in crisis works with the minister to evaluate the remaining choices; the task is to weigh these options against the individual's personal values (money, free time, job, family). If a particular alternative would violate several of his or her values, it can be eliminated as a nonviable alternative. The man who is having financial problems, but values his work in the church, his free time, and family, will certainly reject the idea of a second job as a breach of those values.

After weighing courses of action in terms of values, the minister and the counselee consider each course's potential effectiveness. Will it lead to the chosen goals? After the counselee has considered the potential effectiveness of each alternative, the minister can step in and share information from his or her own experience, or from the experiences of other counselees (always maintaining confidentiality). For example, to a recently divorced man who was isolating himself and yet wanted to meet people, I said that several individuals had found the single-adults group at a neighboring church helpful after their divorces.

After reviewing the various courses of action, individuals in crisis need to choose one or two upon which to embark. Gentle urging on the part of the minister may be required. I frequently find it valuable to write down the commitment on a piece of paper for myself and have counselees write it down as well. They make a covenant to begin doing the chosen alternatives before the next visit, and thus embark on taking small, concrete steps toward achieving their goal.

Committing to Action. After the commitment, action must be immediate. This step is vital because it helps reverse any tendency of ongoing dependence of the counselee on the helper. Action counters the paralysis of crisis and encourages people to do something about their problems, whether they feel like it or not. O. Hobart Mowrer states, "It is easier to act your way into a new way of feeling than to feel your way into a new way of acting" (quoted in Clinebell 1966, 171). Or, in Clinebell's (n.d.) words, "The person's personality or self is like a muscle. When you use a muscle it grows stronger . . . if you don't use the muscle the muscle begins to atrophy and waste away." The resumption of personal control sometimes comes slowly but is accomplished over time.

Helpers need infinite patience. Sometimes people in crisis resist at this point and will "forget" or "not have time" to begin acting on their chosen alternatives. They may be trying to make the helper angry in order to justify breaking off the helping relationship. Such resistance needs to be aired immediately and addressed. Those who are being helped should not be allowed to slide by without at least recognizing their conduct. I repeatedly remind people of their freedom of choice to do or not to do that which will help them with their problems; I will help them to achieve their goals in any way I can but (except in extreme emergencies) will not achieve them for them.

Evaluating. In many ways, review and refinement are not a separate part of all helping, but an ongoing function. Ministers and those they help continually need to evaluate whether the chosen goals and new behaviors are effective toward resolution of the crisis.

In the final sessions of crisis counseling it is always valuable to review the learning that has taken place, encouraging the use of new-found strengths and coping skills for the resolution of future problems and crises, which are certain to occur.

FOLLOW-UP

Follow-up with the person or family in crisis is essential. It deepens the relationship and reaffirms the minister's concern. It determines whether or not they are continuing to do what is needed to resolve their crisis. It communicates that they have a continuing responsibility to do something specific about their problems. Following up does not mean checking up, but showing interest in troubled persons' continued well-being. It also offers an additional chance for the expression of emotions and the assessing of the changes that are being made.

Follow-up also offers ministers a chance to deal with the fallout of a crisis event. Along with leftover feelings of hurt or anger, the gnawing anxiety that "it will happen again" sometimes persists. There may even be another, perhaps more basic, problem for which the person needs to seek counseling help. For example, while putting up a TV antenna on his house, a successful salesman fell from the roof and broke his back. The injury itself triggered a crisis for him and his wife, but as they discussed the problem with their minister it became apparent that they had some serious marital problems. After resolving the initial crisis surrounding the injury, the couple began marriage counseling.

Follow-up does not necessarily take place in the minister's office. A lunch date, a phone call, a stop at someone's shop, a note, or a friendly visit in the home all provide the occasion for seeing if the crisis has been adequately managed.

Having traced some helpful methods of crisis counseling from A to C, including follow-up, we return to the situation of Hector and Donna Mercado. Donna was firm about wanting the divorce and refused marriage counseling. It was evident to the pastor that Hector was under considerable stress. Using Switzer's three criteria for establishing the existence of a crisis, Pastor Cole found:

(1) A recent onset of bad feelings—after six years of marriage, feelings had become overstrained as of the previous Thursday night; (2) The

feelings growing steadily worse—they continued to intensify to the point where Donna forced Hector out of the house and started divorce proceedings, and Hector was now considering suicide; (3) An external event triggering the recent surge of feeling—there had been trouble in the marriage before but it reached a new level of intensity with the Thursday night fight, when Hector called the pastor.

Certain that a crisis was present, Pastor Cole began to apply the A-B-C method of crisis intervention. Three principal steps were used to handle the situation.

Achieving Contact. Pastor Cole already had a relationship with Hector; he had seen him in church regularly. The pastor was not rejecting or judgmental, although Hector feared he might be. If Hector had not had a prior relationship of trust with his minister, he probably would not have sought counsel from anyone.

The pastor practiced most of the attending behaviors. He faced Hector, leaned toward him, and maintained eye contact. Hector responded to the attending behaviors and active listening, and in the second session broke down and sobbed. He felt he was totally without hope. He was cognitively constricted and could see no alternatives other than forcing Donna to live with him or committing suicide. The pastor allowed Hector to tell him the full story, and to lean upon and draw strength from him.

Boiling Down. Focusing the problem was somewhat difficult for the pastor in the second counseling session. Hector cried a great deal. He kept repeating: "If she doesn't come back I'm going to kill myself" and "I want my wife back—that's all I want." It was a long time before any two-way communication could develop. The pastor allowed considerable release of feelings but finally urged that they focus on what Hector could realistically do right away.

Another difficulty was rooted in Pastor Cole's assumption that, because divorce was the precipitating event, it was also the heart of the crisis. With continued listening, however, he was able to boil down the crisis to its central problem: "Hector, if I'm hearing you right, Donna's divorcing you has left you feeling a deep loss and made you very lonely. You don't feel very much like a man." Hector responded, "Yeah, I feel like I've lost my manhood—it's terrible." In these brief summations,

Hector and the pastor developed a *consensual formulation* of the essence of the crisis. They stated it as Hector most sharply experienced it. The crisis of Hector's loss and loneliness had caused within him a severe identity struggle. He relaxed somewhat (and so did Pastor Cole) after they felt they had articulated the crisis at its sharpest point. Sometimes just the process of developing a consensual formulation is all that is needed to turn around a crisis.

In this case, however, the pastor knew that he also had to challenge Hector to cope constructively through concrete action. Before doing so, however, he needed to assess Hector's threats: "You are thinking of suicide? How do you plan on doing it? Do you own a gun? Do you have bullets? Is the gun loaded? Where is it?" (see chap. 4). Pastor Cole found that Hector did have a gun and the ammunition with which to kill himself; the previous night he had even loaded the gun and played with it. He had decided how he would commit suicide, and he had the external means and the inner stress necessary to carry it out. This was a clear indication that Hector's suicide lethality was high and that the pastor would need to respond actively.

Coping Actively. Hector's only goal was to get his wife back. The pastor suggested that this goal did not appear likely, but that he would work with him on it and help him consider alternative ways of achieving it. The pastor inventoried Hector's resources, internal and external, and concluded that he did not have many. He had not faced any severe crises in the past; he had few friends; he did not like his job and was afraid they might fire him if he continued complaining about his problems; he was a dependent person who had never developed an identity of his own. Pastor Cole summarized Hector's three main resources: his work (though he did not like his job, he did like the type of work he was doing); his brother and sister-in-law; and his pastor.

Because of Hector's limited resources, relatively high suicide lethality, and strong dependency, the pastor decided to end the second session by helping him write a calendar of all the things he would do in the three days before they next met: play chess during lunch with a friend at work, take his brother and sister-in-law out for a meal, return to a church school class he used to attend, and the like. He tried to ensure that Hector would be active and involved with people on each of those days. Hector agreed to live by that calendar. He further promised that he would call Pastor Cole at any time, day or night, if he felt he was going to commit suicide.

At the next session, Hector and the pastor discussed ways of reaching the goal of getting Donna to come back. Hector decided that because he had not been "much of a man," he would try to be more independent and autonomous rather than "acting like a baby like I am now." He chose several strategies to accomplish this goal and dedicated himself to them. He became more involved with people, made new friends, joined a community group, and acted more mature among his business associates in specific ways. The pastor challenged him whenever Hector appeared to become overly dependent on him or on others.

Hector chose several alternatives and he acted on them—not all in a week, but within the space of three or four weeks. When he came back to the pastor and said he could not do a task he had committed himself to do, the pastor reflected, "It appears that you want to be led by the hand when we both know you can do it, and do it yourself." The pastor's response was slightly abrasive, but he felt that the relationship could tolerate it. Although Hector was angry, he admitted that he could do it but was afraid. They talked about the fear and role-played ways to handle an uncomfortable situation.

Soon after implementing his courses of action Hector began to change his goal. As he worked through the initial weeks of grief, the former goal of "getting Donna back" evolved into the new goal of "being my own man"—being a more mature adult who, though deeply hurt by the loss of his marriage, wanted to become a better and more self-assured person.

After six sessions (about four weeks) Hector lost his job. Instead of crying over the layoff and threatening suicide, as he had done in his earlier loss, he made up résumés and flew to a trade convention in Chicago where he received several job offers. This experience was gratifying and helped him to realize that he was a competent adult.

After the crisis was resolved, the pastor referred Hector to a self-help group in the church. In the company of other growing persons he continued to develop his skills for healthy interpersonal relationships—and an identity of his own.

REFERRAL

"Properly conceived, referral is a means of using a team effort to help a troubled person. . . . It employs the division-of-labor principle that is the basis of interprofessional cooperation" (Clinebell 1984, 311). There are two types of referral. In one, the helper gives the major responsibility for care over to another professional. This type is frequently necessary when a person in crisis is psychotic, suicidal or homicidal, or needs hospitalization. The other form of referral, more common to the minister doing crisis counseling, involves retaining major responsibility for the care but sending troubled individuals to specialists for specific types of help (for example, to a family debt counselor for assistance with financial planning).

Referral to outside professionals is not a sign of failure. Often it is inevitable. Even if one is a good pastoral carer, a healer, a guide, a reconciler, and a sustainer, it is nevertheless the mark of an effective crisis intervener to know when and how to refer. Referral is a matter of timing, taking into consideration both the state of the person in crisis and the helper's own limitations. Time, skill, and emotional objectivity all play a role in determining when it is best to send a person to more specialized care.

Time

Assuming the pastoral carer has the expertise to deal with a particular person's crisis, it is important to determine whether she or he has the time to handle the situation adequately (and often immediately). One should answer quite frankly: Will I seriously neglect my other responsibilities because of the time given to these individuals? Can I really limit them to only so many minutes or so many sessions per week? Can I honestly and firmly restrict telephone availability? Will such limitations involve a cost to the healing process?

Skill

Even when time is sufficient, in some crisis situations one helper's distinctive complex of skills and experience will be far less helpful to the individual than that of a counselor who has some highly developed facility for dealing with a particular problem. A good illustration is heroin addiction; unless actively working with a drug treatment center, few caregivers are equipped to treat it effectively.

Some questions to ask in determining if a helper has the necessary skills to handle a particular crisis include: Do I feel comfortable working with this person? Can I be sure I am not misinterpreting this person's situation? After perhaps three or four sessions, is the person showing growth? Am I fostering negative dependency?

As a rule of thumb, it is important to consider referring to a mental health professional any person who is or appears to be psychotic, violent, seriously suicidal, homicidal, or whose behavior is noticeably bizarre.

Emotional Objectivity

Even if one has sufficient time and skills that are adequate to a particular problem, it is important to examine one's own emotional objectivity. Because of personal beliefs or values or one's own past difficulties in resolving similar problems, some situations may elicit within the helper feelings of insecurity or hostility, threat or fear. Is this problem one that I have faced but never successfully resolved? Am I so overburdened emotionally because of work and family commitments that I have little left to offer this individual? Do I find myself needing the other's approval so that it is difficult to intervene with integrity and authority? Or am I becoming overly involved emotionally with the person or the situation? If the answer is yes, it is time to refer.

In every phase of the care process, whether in establishing a relationship, working out a course of action, or referring to a specialist, the pastoral carer's effective functioning depends upon the degree to which she or he understands all the limitations of the situation and acts creatively out of a sense of emotional security, stability, and relative objectivity. When referral is required, the following ideas may apply:

• Keep in mind that not everyone will accept suggestions for referral. Some may only want to complain about a situation and not work toward a solution. For others, just talking about the problem and considering a referral is sufficient motivation to action.

• Make referrals in a tactful, concrete way: not, "I think you should see a shrink," but "I'd be happy to recommend several marriage counselors—Dr. Gomez was especially helpful with my sister and I've heard very good things about Dr. Po from several people who have seen her."

• When uncertain of where to refer, call a mental health professional in the congregation, a local crisis line, or an information and referral agency. Explain the situation, and obtain up-to-date information on the person or agency to which one is referring. Sometimes calling the office directly can be helpful in learning whether a waiting list exists, how long it might be, the fee schedule, and any other pertinent information.

• Suggest several referral sources if possible, because one professional may not be immediately available.

• Do not (except in an emergency) make the referral call on behalf of the person in crisis. The individual needs to initiate the call. But it may be helpful to suggest dialing the number immediately or to offer a ride (if you are willing to offer this) to the first appointment.

• Remember that referral is not the first step in the care process, except in an emergency. Establish a relationship, listen carefully to the person's pain, and then slowly, gently begin to nudge toward doing something about the problem, noting how the suggested referral source can benefit the person in the resolution of the crisis.

• After referring, follow up. Call the next day to express in a non-judgmental way, "I called to see how you are today, and to find out if there were any problems in scheduling a session with Dr. Gomez or Dr. Po." If the person gives excuses, ask if there are any further ways to help or if the individual would like to discuss any other things with you. Mention that you will call back in a couple of days to see how things are going. Be as sensitive as is possible neither to hound anyone nor to let him or her shrug off the needed care easily.

The A-B-C method of crisis intervention allows helpers to respond to people in a wide range of situational crises. The *A* of the A-B-C method invites the minister to achieve contact—establish a relationship with the troubled person. The *B* is boiling down the problem to its essentials; it covers responding and focusing the pastoral conversation on the specifics of the crisis. The *C* calls for the person in crisis to cope actively with the difficulty. It includes a five-part problem management method that helps break crisis' paralysis and moves an individual into action. Together these three tasks provide a way that clergy and lay pastoral carers can respond to those in crisis—offering support in their isolation, clarity in their confusion, and direction and hope as they take steps toward a new future.

FOUR

Extreme Interventions

———

For most clergy, crises are a normal part of the work week. People in their care experience bereavement, job loss, discovery of a spouse's infidelity, teenage pregnancy, cancer, abandonment, divorce—and they are thrown into turmoil. At such times they often turn to the pastor for support.

But occasionally ministers are drawn into situations that are not so common, that are tougher, more complex, and even more dangerous than those human crises they face with regularity.

The phone rings at 2 A.M. and the minister stumbles for the receiver. An unfamiliar voice blurts: "You don't know me, but I just wanted to tell someone why I'm doing this. I can't take it anymore. I can't keep living this way. I have fifty Secanols and I've already taken half of them. . . ."

The pastor of a small-town church gets a call from a deputy who tells him that the sheriff is out of town, that the postmaster, a solitary but apparently respectable man, ". . . has gone berserk. He has a gun and he's taken two hostages and he's making all kinds of crazy demands. I know he went to your church once in a while—can you come and talk to him?"

The church's secretary and its female pastor are besieged with a series of obscene and subtly threatening telephone calls by an individual who is often incoherent and expresses a deep hatred of women.

A woman runs into a minister's office in a panic—her daughter and son-in-law (who live next door to the church) have been arguing for three days, and it has suddenly escalated into a violent physical fight.

58

"Would you please do something to stop them before someone gets hurt?"

The A-B-C method of crisis intervention facilitates intervention for most problems that are encountered. But extreme circumstances such as those mentioned above, however rare, cause great concern to those trying to offer care. Threatened homicide, suicide, physical abuse, kidnapping or the taking of a hostage, a grisly death, an explosion at a plant, or the crash of a commercial airplane are typical crisis situations that may call for additional and distinctive modes of intervention.

This chapter touches on such crucial interventions. Included are telephone emergencies, suicide threats, high-risk situations, and threats to the helper's safety.

TELEPHONE CRISIS INTERVENTION

Most telephone conversation is casual and light. It is like dinner table talk; topic after topic comes up and the quality of listening is not always as important as the spirit of telling stories of the day's events. Consequently, it is sometimes difficult for crisis interveners to make the transition from conversational telephone discourse to crisis counseling over the telephone. Even in a dire emergency, habitual ways of responding on the phone may creep into telephone conversation if helpers are not careful. (This is especially likely when the caller has telephoned a number of times before and has repeated roughly the same scenario each time.) The relationship with a caller in crisis is neither social nor antisocial; it must be a working pastoral relationship.

Over-the-phone Crisis Counseling

Face-to-face crisis intervention benefits from nonverbal signals that fill in the meaning behind words. How people position themselves in a chair and gesticulate while talking, their overall demeanor, and especially their facial gestures and eye contact (or lack thereof) aid a helper's understanding of what they are saying. In telephone intervention all these visual data are missing, so helpers need to listen carefully for other nonverbal cues (such as voice tonality, pauses, tension in their speaking, crying or choked sobs). (In addition, because callers cannot get visual or nonverbal cues, helpers must add their own verbal cues in order for callers to realize that they are listening and responding.)

Williams and Douds, social workers at a suicide prevention center, note four features of crisis intervention work over the telephone (Lester and Brockopp 1973, 81). The first is the *greater control* on the part of the person. In face-to-face conversation the troubled person usually has come to the office, waited for the pastor, and learned the amount of time available for the session; therefore the pastor has greater influence than over the phone. In telephone crisis intervention the troubled individual initiates the contact with the helper and may terminate it at any moment. If the helper says anything that the caller perceives as wrong, the caller can hang up.

A second characteristic of telephone counseling is that it allows the *anonymity* of individuals in distress. For some this anonymity gives greater freedom to say what is on their minds; they are more open to conveying over the phone what they would not reveal in a face-to-face encounter.

The third characteristic of crisis phone work is that often the *helper is not known* by the caller. This promotes positive transference; the callers' fantasies of what they want in a caring individual sometimes can be better realized over the phone than in person.

Accessibility is the fourth feature of telephone crisis intervention work. Most individuals have phones and are able to contact a helper whenever they wish. Accessibility is vital in crises, many of which occur outside typical office hours. For example, a great many individuals who threaten suicide do so in the middle of the night. The telephone call may be the only contact they can achieve with someone who will help them make it through the night.

Difficult Calls

Most crisis helpers eventually discover that, for whatever reason, some people who use the phone claim an emergency when none exists. As a working hypothesis, however, the helper must believe persons who say they are in crisis. The truth sometimes is stranger than any bogus situation a caller can invent.

The first task when one receives a telephone call of distress is to find out the person's name, phone number, and address, if possible. This responsibility is so obvious that it is sometimes overlooked. A crisis call may inadvertently be disconnected, and if the helper does not know the caller's name or telephone number, no follow-up can occur. Some years ago a very distraught man threatening suicide called me from a pay phone. While talking he accidentally touched the phone cradle and was cut off. I called him back immediately, and he thanked me. He had used his last coin to make that call and was so upset by one more thing going wrong that he said, "I figured, what's the use, I might as well end it." Most people will give their name and number as an automatic response if it is requested early in the conversation and in a matter-of-fact way. If they refuse, it is best not to force the issue but to continue the conversation and ask again at a later stage.

After getting the name and phone number of the caller, it is also important to determine the parameters of the problem: does the crisis involve other persons, and if so, how many; where are these other persons; are drugs or alcohol involved; are weapons on the premises or have any weapons been used; has there been any abuse or any injuries or threat of injuries; if there have been injuries, how serious are they; and so forth. Some calls, by their very nature, are more difficult and require additional knowledge and preparation. These especially demanding calls include sexual calls, repeat calls, and prank calls.

Most *sexual calls* are not made by persons who want help but are attempts to involve the crisis intervener in their sexual activities. Some call a crisis helper of the opposite sex (or the same sex) and masturbate while telling some story or another; or they may do little more than breathe, making statements such as "Talk to me" or "Don't leave me" or "Let me finish." Tell them directly that if they have a problem to discuss, you are willing to talk with them in the future and then terminate the call.

Most ministers, especially women, have received obscene telephone calls, another type of sexual call. People working on crisis hot lines also get such calls. Again the helper does best to tell such callers that if they want to talk about their problems on another occasion they may do so, and then hang up.

In a third type of sexual call, the caller tries to get the helper into a conversation about sex. Such conversations may begin indirectly but become increasingly more explicit descriptions of sexual activities. These callers may masturbate while recounting their sexual fantasies. One of the simplest ways of differentiating a true sexual problem from a bogus one is to listen for hesitancy or embarrassment on the part of the caller. Most people experience some difficulty talking about sexual problems if they are real. They will stammer or speak haltingly while trying to relate their troubles. Callers who are using the phone to share their sexual fantasies are bolder, and many times will abruptly end the conversation themselves before the crisis intervener has a chance to discontinue it.

Repeat calls are occasionally made by individuals who have such poor personal resources or a lack of insight that they are continually in crisis situations. However, the majority of repeat callers know what they need to do but avoid making decisions and taking action. They talk on the phone as a way to avoid participating in serious counseling or therapy. (In my experience some of these individuals also repeatedly call the church secretary or make frequent visits to the church office.)

It is important to determine whether repeat callers are genuinely asking for help or are avoiding taking responsibility for their problems. Those who lack resources or insight need as much care as the helper has time to offer. (The helper who does not have the time or energy to deal with such calls should refer them to someone else.) The repeat callers who know what they need to do but avoid taking the necessary action require a different response. Ministers should be aware that some repeat callers may contact a number of people in the church; if they do not get the desired response from one person, they will go to the next. Therefore, ministers or leaders of lay pastoral care groups need to keep all helpers alert to these multiple contacts by chronic callers, determine a planned response to them, and inform all helpers of the plan.

With either type of repeat caller it is critical to determine if a real emergency exists. The first type of caller is likely to have a number of real emergencies that call for typical crisis intervention methods. The second type of chronic caller does not usually have a real crisis but only wishes to complain or to vent anger. In any case, it is best to be sure.

The third class of difficult phone calls is *prank calls*. Some people call a helper, pretend they have a problem, and describe it in all its gory detail. After a few minutes, bad acting skills or factual inconsistencies usually make it obvious that this is a prank call and it is time for the helper to put an end to the conversation.

A more difficult prank call is silent. The helper answers the telephone and no one responds at the other end of the line. The problem with silence is that some individuals in crisis are so overwrought that they have trouble putting their pain into words. Without the benefit of visual cues one cannot determine if the quiet on the other end of the line is a trick, or the silence of a person struggling for courage or words to express deep distress.

When a caller is silent, it is best to remain calm and to make statements such as "It's hard to talk about your problems (to someone you don't know)" or "Sometimes it is hard to put into words what you are feeling." One should allow some pauses. After three or four minutes of silence it is usually wise to tell silent callers that when they get to the point where they are able to talk, they should call back. Then hang up.

A final suggestion concerning the use of the telephone in crisis intervention work: not only does the telephone offer accessibility to troubled individuals, it is also a very useful tool for follow-up with those in crisis. Schedules may prevent seeing these persons every day, but phone calls take little time, maintain on-going contact, and allow for an assessment of how they are coping with their problems.

SUICIDE

Whether on the telephone or in a face-to-face conference, one of the most alarming situations a helper will encounter is a person who is or may be suicidal. At such times it is essential to listen for the seriousness of suicide risk—to make judgments about suicide lethality. The assessment of suicide lethality is an additional objective of the B—boiling down and focusing—of the A-B-C method of crisis counseling. The following series of factors can help one gauge the seriousness of suicide threats (Farberow, Heilig, and Litman 1968). The helper should not use these nine basic criteria as a routine checklist but internalize them, obtaining the answers informally but directly in conversation with the potentially suicidal person.

Age and Gender

A person's age and gender is a statistical factor in suicide. Although women more often attempt it, over half (55 percent) of completed suicides are men. The threat of suicide increases in lethality with age, especially among men. Therefore, if both a seventeen-year-old girl and a man in his seventies are threatening suicide, the man is statistically more likely to complete the act—although all talk of suicide must be taken seriously. Suicide among teenagers has risen dramatically in the last thirty years, yet remains statistically lower than for older adults.

Suicide Plan

Is suicide a vague, general threat, or does the person have a specific plan for how to go about it? This is the most critical element in assessing suicide risk. The pastoral carer will have to determine how *specific* is the plan, how *lethal* the method, and how *available* the means for putting the plan into effect. The answers to these questions generally will not be available through just listening, but will require direct and forthright questioning of the troubled person. Some methods of committing suicide are obviously more lethal than others: a gun is more dangerous than tranquilizers, a full bottle of barbiturates more deadly than a handful of aspirin. If a person has a very specific plan, has spent time thinking in detail about how to commit the act, has selected a lethal method, and has the means readily available, the risk of suicide is very serious and requires immediate action on the part of the intervener.

Crisis

People in a crisis occasioned by a loss or impending loss, such as death, divorce, illness, or retirement, account for many serious threats of suicide. A number of people in crisis will consider suicide as one possible way of coping with the adversity. If the distress is extreme and the individual has a specific suicide plan, then the helper must respond even more actively.

Symptoms

Suicide can occur as a result of several different emotional states, among them depression, psychosis, and agitation. The most serious is the depressed-agitated state, in which a person feels emotionally depressed but is simultaneously tense and active and therefore possesses the energy and determination necessary to complete the act. Contrary to popular myth, however, not everyone who commits suicide is depressed.

Other categories of individuals at risk for suicide are the recently bereaved or divorced, alcoholics and other substance abusers, male homosexuals, and sexual deviates. Each of these groups has a relatively high suicide rate.

Meaning and Religious Involvement

People who are neither influenced by nor committed to any religious group or belief system are freer to complete the act of suicide. Strong religious beliefs and regular involvement with some church or religious group provide both emotional support and social constraint against suicide. Nevertheless, even deeply religious people sometimes take their own lives.

Resources

Although people who are suicidal may feel they have no resources, that nobody cares, the pastoral carer knows that usually more resources are available than they realize. It is essential to identify relatives, friends, church members, social workers, coworkers, and others who are available to assist suicidal individuals through their crisis. Above all, encourage them to be frank with others about the seriousness of their difficulties. In the case of one who appears suicidal and seems immobilized, it may be a good idea to inform some resource persons of the suicide potential so they can become involved and actively communicate their caring. When people who are considering suicide have (or perceive they have) few personal resources, then the pastor and lay pastoral carers—as the representative presence of the church—can reach out to them, broadening their network of resources and providing support as they grapple with their predicament.

Life-style

A relatively stable life-style—perceivable by indicators like consistent work history, long marriage and enduring family relations, and absence of past suicide activity—provides some measure of deterrence from suicide. Unstable individuals may exhibit chronic addiction, job-hopping or marriage-hopping, character disorder or psychosis, frequent unresolved crises, and so on. Chronic suicide threats happen only among unstable personalities, but acute suicidal gestures may occur among people with either stable or unstable life-styles.

Communication

The individual who has stopped communicating with others may have given up hope and is more likely to attempt suicide. Indirect, nonverbal communication that one is having thoughts of ending life (making a new will, giving up prized possessions or favorite activities, and so forth) is as important as direct verbal threats; unfortunately, indirect communication seldom reaches helping professionals. Family and friends may be the only ones to notice such signs of distress, and they can provide the pastor or mental health professional with information regarding the lethality of the threat. Sometimes, tragically, no one notices. By maintaining contact with key laypersons, pastors may hear of people whose behavior indicates they are at risk, and then seek them out before they act on their suicide impulses.

Medical Fears

The helper should determine if a suicidal individual has (or fears) a serious disease, such as cancer, AIDS, a chronic illness, or an impending or recent surgery. Individuals with terminal illness may be attracted to suicide as a way of coping with or avoiding pain. Some people have committed suicide believing they had cancer when in fact they did not.

With the exception of a specific and lethal plan, none of the above criteria is necessarily dangerous when taken alone. It is important to gather all the information and look at the whole picture to see if a pattern is beginning to form.

Take all ideas about suicide seriously. This is the basic underlying rule in dealing with suicide, even the hint of it. When a person says, "I'm tired of trying," "Life isn't worth living anymore," "There is no way out," or the like, the minister should ask directly if she or he is contemplating suicide. It simply is not true that talking about suicide will encourage a person to do it; talking about it in frank and specific detail (so that one can offer assistance) is much better than ignoring it. Whenever there is even the slightest hint of such a possibility, the assessment of suicide lethality is a necessary addition to the B—boiling down—phase of crisis counseling.

HIGH-RISK CRISIS SITUATIONS

There are certain occasions when helpers find themselves offering care in extremely difficult situations: people who are suicidal, enraged, mentally disturbed, or potentially violent; domestic disputes; kidnapping or hostage taking, and the like. All involve extra risk, and all call for extra measures. Ministers will want to opt out of some of these situations—and should opt out, if they can pass to a more appropriate intervener—but it is possible to find oneself in the middle of a high-risk situation and have no choice but to act.

In such cases helpers' first concern must be for their own personal safety (discussed in detail at the end of this chapter). This is no time for heroics. If at all possible one should get assistance and work as part of a team. Sharing the burden with other helpers gives one time to think about responses, to avoid overreacting, and to benefit from other perspectives. Collaborative efforts in high-risk crises are best for both the helper and the person in crisis.

Developing Relationships

The following are suggestions for structuring relationships and negotiating decisions in demanding circumstances. In volatile situations some approaches work best for developing relationships with people who have probably had poor interpersonal relationships in the past.

Establishing rapport with people who are threatening suicide or who are violent requires more finesse on the part of crisis interveners. They have to be able to develop relationships with a wide range of individuals: street people, corporate lawyers, revivalists hawking tracts on corners, rednecks, people who live in elegant and expensive homes, counterculture freaks, middle-class retirees, prisoners, prostitutes, gardeners, entertainers—an endless variety of human beings. Helpers sometimes have a very narrow range of people they can effectively counsel, that is, people like themselves: middle class, educated, religiously sensitive, and motivated. Helpers who are uncomfortable with people different from themselves need to uncover their limitations and stretch themselves, developing a capacity to relate to a wider spectrum of human experience.

How ministers go about establishing a relationship with people in crisis is particularly important in high-risk situations. Interveners must exercise great flexibility in the way they position themselves in relation to persons in distress. They must listen carefully for clues that will tell them how the troubled ones want to define the relationship. (For example, potentially violent individuals with a background in crime, though acting aggressively, may still see themselves as having little worth. Thus they may distrust helpers who treat them with deference; they may be more comfortable with the helper taking a slightly superior posture in the relationship.) The most common mistake is to act as if the person in crisis is a close friend. Sometimes when helpers are uncomfortable or frightened they act overly friendly; such warmth and friendliness may be more than a troubled person has ever experienced and may be doubted.

Using the Right Words

One of the first tasks in establishing a relationship in difficult situations is to determine how to address troubled persons. What do they want to be called? The helper can simply ask, "What is your name?" or "What shall I call you?" (It is best not to address individuals by their first names unless they request it. Such references may suggest an insincere chumminess and lead to mistrust.) If they do not give a name, refer to them as "you." After the conversation has progressed, say, "I'm a little uncomfortable just saying 'you.' Would you be willing to tell me your name or a name I may use?"

While most crisis situations may allow the intervener some margin for error in address, speech patterns, or phrasing, in highly volatile circumstances a small detail like the helper's word choices can make or break the relationship. Phrases that can block effectiveness include the royal "we," as in: "We all get angry at our children." Many individuals find "we" condescending, particularly if they interpret it as meaning "you." It is also good to avoid absolutes, terms like "always," "any," "all," or "never."

Another less-than-helpful phrase that I have heard crisis interveners use is: "That is all I am asking of you." Such a statement sounds patronizing and may prompt a negative reaction. "Would you mind . . ." or other tentatively stated requests also may backfire. For example, a person threatening suicide calls and indicates she has barbiturates; if you respond by saying "Would you mind bringing the pills to my office?" she might well think or even say, "Yes, I would mind."

Perhaps due to poor childhood relationships with their parents, many individuals in high-risk circumstances are hypersensitive to what they perceive as condescending language or demeaning ways of talking to them. Therefore helpers must avoid expressing themselves in parental ways—neither scolding nor cheering up (which only serves to discount the pain and suffering of the depressed or distressed).

Finally, helpers need to be careful not to use religious or psychological buzzwords. Anxious individuals may not understand such jargon, and it may cause them to become even more confused, upset, or enraged.

Defusing Volatile Situations

The good news for pastoral carers who are anxious about facing a "bad news" crisis is that some methods tend to be effective at defusing emotions and restoring stability in high-risk circumstances. One such technique is sometimes useful in discussing alternative courses of action with those who are greatly upset and is called the "illusion of alternatives" (Everstine and Everstine 1983). Most parents have used this ploy with their children: "Which vegetable would you prefer for supper, peas or broccoli?" The parents appear to give the children a choice (peas or broccoli) but the parents determine the alternatives; they do not offer the choice of not eating vegetables. Likewise, when an agitated or suicidal individual needs to be taken to a hospital for review and possible confinement, the illusion of alternatives may serve well: "Would you like me to arrange for the police to take you or would you rather have a family member drive you there?" The helper does not give the choice of going or not going to the hospital for an evaluation, having determined (with appropriate consultation) that such an evaluation is essential. Most people who are given transportation options will choose one of them—usually a relative—to deliver them to the hospital. This method is not without danger, but intervention in very demanding situations sometimes requires risky methods.

Another useful technique in difficult situations is acting slightly confused when responding to a highly upset individual. I will sometimes say, "I want to make certain that I understand you correctly," and then repeat back what I heard in a slightly inaccurate way. Most people want to make certain they are understood properly, and thus upset persons may rechannel their energy from explosive outbursts to explanations of what they are saying.

A similar procedure is reframing. There are several different reframing techniques; in one method the minister defuses a potentially explosive situation by placing a more favorable frame or connotation on the actions of one or more of the combatants. For example, if a woman has accused her volatile husband of being a workaholic who is "never home, doesn't care to spend time with the family, is only interested in his career," I may suggest that his attention to his work reveals that he is very concerned about his family's comfort and financial well-being, and is a good provider. This is not a Pollyanna response nor is it the power of positive thinking. It is a restructuring of the situation to highlight positives that are truly present in what the troubled persons have said or done.

Oddly enough, humor is another useful technique in high-risk situations; it has a way of disarming people in crisis, diverting their attention from what is upsetting them. I am not suggesting that jokes need to be told or that any insensitivity be communicated. Persons in crisis must never be the butt of a joke—if there is one, the helper takes that role. Once again, such an approach has some degree of risk; nevertheless, if there is something comic in the situation, a little laughter may help break the tension.

It is important to note that, in general, therapeutic maneuvers or counseling techniques that are useful in one's office may be inappropriate when visiting people in their homes. When helpers leave their offices they give up some of their professional persona and authority, and they need to act more tentatively. Consequently, some of the confrontive or assertive interventions that could be accomplished easily in the pastor's office are not as easily accomplished in a person's living room.

Discerning Perceptions of the Helpers

Most helpers are good, positive, well-meaning people—solid members of the church and of the community. They consider themselves non-threatening, caring individuals genuinely interested in giving comfort. But people who are threatening harm to others or vowing to take their own lives may not see the helper in the same light. They may have spent most of their lives reacting to others who tell them what to do; they may have had no experience with one who is genuinely interested in them. Therefore, do not assume that a troubled person will perceive you as the compassionate, helpful, earnest person you might be in the eyes of others.

Quick Action Requiring Careful Thought

Immediate action is essential in crisis intervention work. Yet, when responding to the crucial situations described in this chapter, helpers must give themselves time to think about what to say and how to respond.

Know how you typically respond in tense or crisis situations. Do you talk too little or too much? Many helpers compensate for their own anxiety by asking too many questions. This may be counterproductive because many distressed people have spent much of their lives answering questions of people in authority, and they do not like it. When I face a tricky circumstance my natural tendency is to move at a faster pace, to talk and act more quickly. The exact opposite is usually needed. I have to slow down my reactions (which may have been speeded up by my anxiety); I must give myself time to think before I act. Lives may depend upon it.

PERSONAL SAFETY

Most people are neither used to getting beaten or slapped around nor accustomed to being around people who are perpetually under the influence of alcohol and other drugs. In most congregations, clergy work among a milder sort of humanity. As a result, caregivers may fail to take the necessary personal safety precautions when responding to crises. In 99 percent of the situations ministers encounter, this naïveté will create no problem. In a small fraction of instances, however, crisis interveners must act with caution. Frightened or angry people who feel trapped may act in ways that are utterly foreign to most helpers' experience.

The first edition of this book did not include a section on the protection of the helper. I now believe safety is an important element of crisis counseling. Perhaps it is my age; perhaps it is the memory of being in dangerous circumstances on several occasions. Or it may be my knowledge of several ministers who were threatened (in two cases, injured) that has caused me to pay more attention to personal protection. The following considerations need to become elements of intervention in crises, especially in hazardous or volatile contexts.

If at all possible, do not go to the scene of an emergency situation; it is much better to arrange for a neutral site or office visit. When telephone calls come at night it is usually better to talk people through a situation on the phone than to go to the scene. Arranging for a family member or friend to stay through the night with an individual who is suicidal and making an appointment for the following morning is often sufficient. In addition, one good approach is to develop a contract with such persons in which they pledge not to do anything to harm themselves between the time of the call and the next morning's session.

But sometimes, day or night, helpers must go to the scene of a serious crisis. The following are suggestions for such occasions.

Do *not* go to the site of such situations alone, especially at night. Police officers usually ask for backup when called to critical situations. They know, for example, that each year more police officers are injured responding to domestic disputes than in any other circumstance. If the possibility of harm exists, ministers should simply not go, at least not without assistance.

Before such crises occur it is good for ministers to have chosen particular individuals who can respond to a call for assistance at a moment's notice. Members of self-help groups such as Alcoholics Anonymous are especially valuable; they are used to getting up in the middle of the night to help others in difficulty. Do not hesitate to call on the police for assistance; in fact, if a weapon or physical violence is involved, their presence is vital. It has been my experience that police will seldom give a minister a hard time for overreacting. One officer responded to my apologies by saying, "I'd rather have you err in the direction of calling me when there is no danger than to err in not calling me when there is danger. Then I have two problems. I have to separate the disputants *and* I have to try to protect you from danger."

When driving to the scene, park several houses away so that a slow, cautious approach to the house can be made, listening for sounds and keeping an eye out for any disturbances. Move cautiously to the door and listen some more. After knocking, stand back and off to the side of the door to keep out of the way in case anyone comes bursting through it. When someone answers the door, introduce yourself, but do not enter the house unless invited. If the person at the door asks you in, but someone inside tells you to leave, then stay outside or leave. By now, the situation described on the phone may have radically changed. The caller expressed only one view of the situation; others may be displeased or angry at the call; they do not want you involved.

When entering a room, move slowly. Scan it, looking for signs of violence: broken furniture, glass, or evidence that people have been fighting. Look also for weapons. If the room is dark, enter with even greater caution, and ask for permission to turn on a light. Once inside, attempt to keep all disputants in front of you and in view, not letting anyone get behind you. Urge family members to sit down and not leave the room, unless you are separating the disputants and sending one of them to another room with another helper.

Try to be the one who chooses where conversations will take place. Even though the kitchen is a comfortable place where people can sit over a cup of coffee and talk informally, it is not the place to be in dangerous situations. There are too many potential weapons in a kitchen. The bedroom is another bad idea—it is where most people store their firearms. The dining room or living room are safer sites for conversation in potentially violent crises.

Gain control of the emergency situation in any way possible without becoming physically involved. One of the first tasks is to get everyone seated; there is less danger when people are less mobile. Be sure to sit down with the others; to remain standing while others are seated may be the body language of a negative authority figure. Choose a hard-backed chair, if possible, thus avoiding the chance of taking someone's favorite chair. It is a good idea to sit near an outside door so that if hostilities flare again, a quick exit is possible.

Do not feign heroism. If the situation appears to be beyond your abilities, or if you become concerned about your own or another's safety, then leave immediately and get help. Once again, it never hurts to call in police for assistance if the crisis is beyond your control. In many communities helpers can inform the police of the visit beforehand and ask them to wait nearby; in any case it is good to have an existing relationship with the local police in order to avoid needing to explain who you are in the heat of a crisis.

Finally, however skilled at establishing relationships, however prepared with techniques of high-risk intervention, and however cautious in dangerous circumstances, sometimes the best treatment pastoral carers can offer individuals in crisis is to direct them to others, to professionals who specialize in the types of care that will best meet their needs. This point applies especially to difficult or dangerous situations; in cases such as this chapter described, referral is often essential.

Chapter 3 gave a detailed description of referral. The pastoral carer who is unsure about the best course in one of these tough crises, or who recognizes the need for some specific outside skill or resource, must view referral not as an admission of incompetence but as a skillful professional act. It may be the sane and unheroic deed that saves a human life.

FIVE

Portraits in Crisis

Crises are not all alike. That seems obvious but nonetheless deserves mention, because in developing techniques for managing crises one may be tempted to overlook the uniqueness of each individual human situation. An obvious danger is that what worked to resolve one crisis may fail in the next. But crises have common themes and experiences, and they do form clusters that share sufficient characteristics to make their study fruitful.

Caplan, Mason, and Kaplan (1965, 151), researchers in the field of crisis theory, believe that crises differ in two ways: according to whether they are developmental or situational; and according to the type of challenge or hazard involved, such as death of a loved one or a significant personal injury. They found that, despite a diversity of precipitators, within any cluster of crisis types some psychological tasks appear to occur regularly and repeatedly. The precipitators of crises can be as varied as the people who experience them, yet there are some basic dynamics at the core of every crisis. Were this not the case, we would not be able to study crisis intervention in general, but only the dynamics and treatment of specific cases.

As a way of demonstrating the applicability of generalized crisis theory to a multiplicity of situations, this chapter describes several different cases of people in crisis, and shows how the A-B-C method of crisis intervention was used in each case. I suggest that readers project themselves into the situation and not only think about how to counsel the person in each case—there is no one best way—but also try to define the precipitator of the crisis, the individual's perception of it, and, with the details presented, a consensual formulation for the person.

74

A CASE OF ATTEMPTED SUICIDE

Pastor Kurt Anderson was exhausted from all the activities of a usual Sunday—two services, a special church council meeting in the afternoon, and the youth group that evening. It was close to midnight when he went to bed. Within minutes, just as he began to slide into that delightful phase halfway between waking and sleeping, the telephone rang.

The caller was Rick Patton, age forty-seven, phoning about his forty-five-year-old wife, Rebecca. They had been married over twenty years and had no children. Pastor Anderson had never met or talked with the couple before.

Immediate Situation

The speech at the other end of the line was excited and rapid. Rick blurted, "My wife has taken a lot of pills—I don't know what to do." The crisis precipitator for Rick was the threatened (and potentially real) loss of the most significant relationship in his life. He perceived the potential loss as disastrous. His coping methods were temporarily paralyzed. He had done nothing for the first five minutes; then he thought of calling Pastor Anderson, whose name had been given to him four weeks before when the couple moved from Wisconsin to Florida.

Intervention

Before Pastor Anderson was able to intervene, he had to deal with his own feelings. The adrenaline flowed through his body, and he found himself asking mainly informational questions of Rick. For the first minute or two the pastor too was paralyzed; he had read what to do in a suicide situation and he had counseled several people who had threatened suicide, but this was his first experience with someone who had actually done something destructive to herself. Just as Pastor Anderson's anxiety eased a bit and he felt better able to cope with the situation, the caller thrust the phone into his wife's hand. So far Pastor Anderson had learned who the caller was (name and address) and what he was calling about. He had asked what the drug was (Secanol), how many were taken (remainder of bottle, number unknown), and when (five or ten minutes previously).

But when Rebecca Patton took the phone she was able only to mumble incoherently. Pastor Anderson could not understand what she was saying. He tried yelling into the phone to arouse her. Then he heard a thud and the clunk of the receiver as it hit the floor. Evidently she had collapsed into unconsciousness.

Kurt Anderson had been on the phone now for four or five minutes. He had little time to develop a relationship. He realized that he had to take a directive role. When Rick came back to the phone screaming that his wife had passed out, Kurt said, "OK. Here is what we are going to do." The pastor could not wait for Rick to mobilize his coping abilities; he gently but firmly gave orders.

Pastor Anderson first told Rick to make sure that his wife's breathing passage was not blocked and that she was still breathing. Then he told him to leave their phone connection open, go to a neighbor's house and call 911, tell the neighbor what had happened, and enlist help. Rick balked at this suggestion, saying he had only been in town a short time and did not know his neighbors. Pastor Anderson responded, "Listen, your wife's life is in danger—don't worry about things like that. People are usually willing to help in a time of crisis."

After two or three minutes that seemed like an eternity, Rick returned to the phone. He had made the call and had enlisted the help of a married couple who lived next door; a police car was already pulling up in front, and Rick had to hang up. Pastor Anderson requested that Rick call him from the hospital.

At 1:30 A.M. Pastor Anderson's phone rang again. Rick said the ambulance had arrived very quickly, his wife's stomach was pumped, and the doctor said she was going to be all right. Pastor Anderson suggested that she needed to see a counselor immediately upon discharge from the hospital. Rick said she had already made an appointment to see a psychologist, but that appointment was still two weeks away. Pastor Anderson let him know that most psychotherapists will see a person sooner if a crisis exists, and he strongly recommended that Rick call the psychologist the first thing in the morning. Rick agreed to do so.

Follow-up

Early Monday afternoon Pastor Anderson called Rick. He learned that Rebecca was already out of the hospital and was seeing the psychologist that very afternoon. Pastor Anderson told Rick to call him if he could be of any further help. Later that week, he stopped by their home to invite them to church and see about other ways he could assist them with their move to town.

Observations

It is obvious from this case that active intervention was absolutely necessary. The pastor temporarily took responsibility for and control of the situation—he gave orders. Fortunately Rick trusted the pastor enough to follow these orders—a good example of the lowered level of defensiveness and heightened psychological accessibility a person experiences in a crisis. Few people would be so trusting of a stranger in ordinary circumstances.

Kurt's questions to Rick about the attempted suicide were specific: "With what?" "How much? "How long ago?" Getting exact information and precise details are always important in a suicidal crisis so that an appropriate intervention can be shaped from the information (chap. 4). Finally, the pastor told Rick to call 911 (the fire department should be called if there is no 911 emergency number) rather than an ambulance because he knew that in their city, as in many cities, the 911 dispatcher automatically notifies the fire department, the police, and an ambulance in a suicide attempt. As a result three sources of help were soon rushing to the scene. (If he had call waiting on his phone, Pastor Anderson would have made the call himself.)

A CASE OF ALZHEIMER'S DISEASE

Dorothy and Clint Jacobson were lifelong members of a Lutheran church in a small northwestern Wisconsin town. Dorothy had retired early from her teaching career to take care of her husband. Their pastor, Janice Rue, knew that Clint had been diagnosed as having Alzheimer's disease. Pastor Rue visited the Jacobsons regularly and offered her help or that of the congregation, but Dorothy always refused. She was obviously embarrassed about her husband's condition. The Jacobsons belonged to the school of thought that "a family takes care of its own."

Immediate Situation

Dorothy went to a neighbor's house to borrow several eggs for some baking, got into a conversation, and was delayed ten or fifteen minutes. When she returned home, her husband was gone. Dorothy was not concerned at first; he would sometimes wander out to the garage and tinker. But this time he was not there. After checking with neighbors and still not locating him, she became worried that he had walked into the nearby woods, and she called the police. She also called Pastor Rue.

Intervention

The police, members of the church, and people in the community searched for Clint Jacobson all afternoon and evening to no avail. Pastor Rue alternated spending time with Dorothy, searching in the woods, and calling members of her congregation and several neighboring ones for additional help.

Clint Jacobson was found early the next morning—cold, dehydrated, and hungry—over eight miles from his house. Everyone breathed a sigh of relief. He was hospitalized for observation and released in good health the next day.

Dorothy was at her wits' end after Clint came home from the hospital. Everyone was excited and congratulated her (and themselves) for finding him, but she now knew she had a sizable problem on her hands. She could never again leave Clint alone.

The months and perhaps years of taking care of Clint twenty-four hours a day, as he would increasingly lose mental facilities and even urinary control, stretched out before Dorothy. Their two daughters lived in distant cities. Dorothy was not in the habit of asking for help. But she also was not able to handle the strain of caring for her husband day in, day out.

Janice Rue realized that Dorothy was crumbling under the strain of caring for her husband. Clint's walk in the woods was the last straw; Dorothy's fear of losing him had paralyzed her. She could hardly prepare a meal for herself or her husband, and had slept little in three days when Janice Rue finally intervened. Alone with Pastor Rue, Dorothy began to shake physically and had difficulty stopping.

Janice Rue sat with Dorothy and told her that she obviously had to make changes. Dorothy agreed that things could not go on as they had been. She also agreed that she could no longer hide Clint's illness from the neighbors.

Over the next four or five days, Pastor Rue worked as an advocate, a strong voice for change, and a compassionate listener. She sat down with Dorothy and her daughters, who had flown in during the crisis, and as a group they made some decisions concerning Clint's care. Clint was still capable of passing pleasurable moments with Dorothy in their home, and the family decided to delay placing him in a nursing home (even though they knew it would soon be necessary). Instead they planned ways in which Dorothy could get relief while he remained at home.

Pastor Rue asked a member of the congregation, an attorney and trust officer in a local bank, to handle the legal issues that resulted from Clint's deteriorating mental abilities. In addition, she worked with the chair of the church's lay pastoral care team to arrange for people to relieve Dorothy so she could get out of the house on a regular basis; she also helped Dorothy begin the process of obtaining assistance from government agencies for Clint's care.

Follow-up

With the active intervention of the pastor, members of the congregation, and the local community, the crisis of Clint's disappearance and Dorothy's exhaustion was turned around. Eight months after Clint's walk in the woods, his deterioration reached the point where he had to be admitted to an extended care facility. That was another loss for both of the Jacobsons, but this time they had planned in advance for the change.

Observations

This crisis not only had a dramatic precipitator (Clint's disappearance) but was complicated by Dorothy's exhaustion; she could no longer handle the strain of the constant care she gave to Clint. Up to that point life with Clint had already become a series of minor and sometimes not-so-minor incidents in which Clint did something dangerous to himself or to others, but this final event pushed her to the edge and helped her recognize that change was required.

Marion Roach has stated that "Alzheimer's disease is a disease of separation" (1987, 14). As the person dissolves, family members find themselves increasingly separated from their loved one. It places tremendous burdens upon patients and family members alike. They can expect an evolution in roles, in the ways they relate to each other interpersonally, emotionally, and intellectually, and in their plans for the future. The progressive nature of Alzheimer's disease obstructs and eventually prevents the patient's active participation in family decisions and the charting of the future.

The care of a person suffering from Alzheimer's disease exacts a considerable psychological and physical toll, and there is the potential for a series of crises over the years until death comes. The crisis can be precipitated by a dramatic event like the patient wandering off, but it can also come when the coping methods and resources of the family are exhausted and a minor incident occurs—an exhaustion crisis.

A CASE OF LOST JOB SECURITY

Dennis Jackson, an eighteen-year-old junior college freshman, was carrying a course load of seventeen hours and working twenty hours a week for an employment agency. During high school he was very involved in youth activities at church, and had known the youth pastor since early adolescence. He was living with his parents. Dennis was interested in getting at least a two-year associate of arts degree and taking general courses while deciding on his future. His pastor, Michelle Rand, considered him a well-adjusted person who was mature beyond his years. Dennis was engaged and planned to be married in about two years.

Immediate Situation

Two weeks before Dennis sought the pastor's counsel, Mr. Carlton, office manager at the employment agency where Dennis worked, quit and went to another company. Mr. Carlton then asked Dennis to quit also and come to work for him. Dennis was excited about this possibility at first, especially since he had begun to feel disappointed with his new office manager, who was talking about "making some personnel changes around here." Both Dennis's parents and his fiancée noticed that he was beginning to show anxiety and was expressing dislike for his new boss. At times he felt almost paranoid: his hours were being cut, he was being "put down," and he wanted to quit. Mr. Carlton had made grand promises concerning salary, travel allowance, vacation time, and future advancement; but when Dennis began getting serious about a possible change, Mr. Carlton hedged a bit on some of these promises—though "they'd certainly be considered" when Dennis went full-time with the new company. Dennis was not even sure whether the position with Mr.

Carlton would be permanent. He had reservations, and feelings of uncertainty quickly mounted. He started to panic.

Dennis's crisis was stimulated by a loss of job security. He felt he was no longer valued at his present position, and felt insecure when Mr. Carlton's promises grew vague. By the time he sought out Pastor Rand, Dennis was grieving over the loss of a secure and happy job situation. His coping methods appeared exhausted. He was requesting help from everyone, including his fiancée and parents, and receiving conflicting advice.

Intervention

The night Dennis called Pastor Rand he had been struggling ineffectively all evening to write a term paper. He was so paralyzed by indecision about the job that it was affecting his schoolwork. Dennis told the pastor that he had problems and asked if they could sit down and talk as soon as possible. Pastor Rand arranged to see him between school and work the next day.

When Dennis arrived in Pastor Rand's office he was clearly at wit's end. The pastor was empathetic, and allowed him to tell the whole story. Dennis was pleased with the good relationship he had with his former boss, Mr. Carlton, but he also raised some questions about the advisability of a change: Were conditions really that bad where he was presently employed? Were not his feelings of being put down simply a reaction to his new manager's insecurity? Would he be willing to talk with the branch manager about his relationship to the company? Dennis also asked questions about the basic economics of the job change, especially the greater traveling distance.

After Dennis told his story Pastor Rand helped him to boil down the many facets of his problem. The pastor stated their consensual formulation: "What I hear you saying is that you feel paralyzed. You've had a good working relationship with your ex-boss, but since he left you've felt less happy, more anxious and concerned. You're in a dilemma, not knowing whether you should go to work for Mr. Carlton, given all the uncertainties and the greater distance to travel, or stay in your present job where you feel you might not be able to work with the new supervisor."

Dennis blurted out, "What do I do now?" Pastor Rand suggested that they needed more information before he began to act. Dennis

agreed to see the general manager, Mr. Warner, and share his predicament before deciding what to do. Pastor Rand also suggested that
Dennis obtain more data on the new job possibility, try to nail things
down with his former employer, and come back in a couple of days to
review the new information.

Two days later Dennis walked into Pastor Rand's office noticeably
more upset. He had talked with Mr. Warner about his relationship with
the new office manager, but instead of listening and being supportive,
Mr. Warner reprimanded Dennis for coming to him without first discussing the matter with his new supervisor—and accused him of being
overly suspicious and looking for trouble. The office manager had evidently told Mr. Warner some things about Dennis that were untrue,
and Dennis saw right away that any defensive responses on his part
would have no credibility. Mr. Carlton was also of little help, and Dennis
began to suspect that he was not entirely secure in his new position.

Dennis's predicament now appeared worse; he thought he had al-
ienated his present employer beyond reconciliation, and saw Mr. Carlton's carrot shriveling before his eyes. Pastor Rand felt at this point it
was imperative for Dennis to list all his options, not just the two he
had presented at the outset, and to weigh them in terms of his values
and goals. Some of Dennis's alternatives included looking for another
job; trying to get a loan so he could quit working and concentrate on
his studies; apologizing profusely to his present employer and "knuck-
ling under" to the new regime; and accepting Mr. Carlton's offer despite
its many uncertainties.

Dennis's education emerged as his dominant value and goal in this
situation, and he evaluated all alternatives in the light of his return to
effective functioning in school. But money, and a possible future career
in personnel work, were issues he could not ignore. After weighing all
possible courses of action, Dennis and Pastor Rand arrived at a compromise that he agreed to try for two months. Dennis would continue
in his present position and turn down his former boss's offer. This would
at least eliminate the immediate pressure of decision making. He would
attempt to be considerate of his new boss (here Pastor Rand helped to
pinpoint specific behaviors Dennis could improve) and to achieve a
degree of acceptance of things as they were until the semester break,
when he would have time to look for another job without disrupting

his studies. Dennis resigned himself to staying in his present post, "making the best of a bad situation," until summer if need be.

Follow-up

Once Dennis had embarked upon a course of action, Pastor Rand extracted from him a promise to call her weekly to share his progress. She urged that he refrain from seeking advice from so many sources; it was only confusing him. Dennis heartily agreed.

In subsequent meetings—over the telephone and in person—Pastor Rand was able to help Dennis understand the difficulty of being a boss over a part-time employee who obviously knew more about the business than he did—and was probably more intelligent as well. Sometimes Dennis just vented his frustrations, but usually the pastor was able to help him see how some small act on his part could make him seem less threatening to his supervisor, and therefore make his life at work more tranquil.

Observations

Pastor Rand knew Dennis well enough to recognize ways in which he was probably irritating his new supervisor, and she was not afraid to point those out to him. In the vulnerability of his crisis, Dennis did not resist her suggestions. A new job did not materialize at semester break, but by then Dennis was functioning well and was content to wait for the right position to open up—understanding that few jobs are free of interpersonal stress and perhaps none is ideal.

Dennis's crisis was not resolved through any significant external change in his environment or circumstances; what did change was Dennis's perception of the situation and his active utilization of coping mechanisms designed to keep his life on an even keel so he could concentrate on what he valued most.

A CASE OF A CHILD'S REACTION TO A MOVE

Pastor Sally Carpenter was an assistant minister at a large downtown church in a midwestern city. She was responsible for Christian education and also served as counselor for the church's parochial school.

On many mornings Pastor Carpenter would walk through the halls of the school, greeting and being greeted by the children as they arrived.

One Monday morning Patty, a six-year-old in the first grade, greeted Pastor Carpenter as usual and then added, "I have some bad news to tell you." When Pastor Carpenter asked what it was, Patty said: "My father has left home for a while." The pastor asked why, and Patty replied: "Because he has to work out of town."

Pastor Carpenter did not know Patty's parents well. Patty had two brothers attending the school—Matthew, eight, and Peter, eleven. She was shy but always greeted Pastor Carpenter with a smile. Patty did not seem very upset that morning, and the pastor continued walking down the hall greeting other children.

Immediate Situation

The next day, Patty's teacher came to Pastor Carpenter's office and related the following series of incidents: On the day before, Patty also had told him that her father had "gone away for a while." He did not pursue it because it did not seem to bother her, but that morning Patty asked the school secretary to call him out of the lounge before school started. Patty told her teacher that her father had come back home but "he doesn't love me anymore." When the teacher asked why she said that, Patty replied that her father had beaten her with his hand. The teacher brought her to the school nurse, who could find no signs of a beating. Throughout that morning Patty told the teacher one story after another, each more fantastic than the last: "The house burned down," "My mother almost died last night." Whenever the teacher discredited a story, Patty simply said she was kidding and laughed.

This behavior was atypical for Patty, who was generally rather withdrawn. Finally, just before lunch, Patty began to cry and said her stomach hurt and she felt sick. When the teacher asked if she wanted to go home, she screamed that she had no home and hated everybody, especially her father. The teacher brought Patty to the nurse's office and sought the assistance of Pastor Carpenter.

Intervention

After Pastor Carpenter and the teacher talked for a few minutes, they went down to the nurse's office to meet Patty. Pastor Carpenter related to Patty that her teacher had told her all the fantastic tales she had been telling, and asked "Is something bothering you?" Responding to the pastor's skill in empathetically talking with children, Patty finally opened up. During the past weekend her family had moved from their apartment to a house. For the parents it was an exciting move because they were finally in their own home. It appeared, however, that no one in the family had taken the time to tell Patty anything about the move or why it was necessary. The loss of a familiar environment and of her friends in the apartment building was too much for Patty to cope with. Her sense of security was threatened. She viewed her father as the culprit, because he was the one who physically moved her things.

Patty was very close to her brother Matt, and the teacher suggested that Matt come to their class that afternoon. Her other brother, Peter, joined them as well. The brothers shared information about the move with Patty and the other children. The teacher also read stories about moving, and the entire class shared in Patty's experience. Patty discovered that two children in her class now lived a few houses away from her.

Meanwhile, Pastor Carpenter called the mother, explained the situation, and offered to stop by, but the mother was too embarrassed about their messy house to have a visitor. Pastor Carpenter suggested that the family, especially the father, talk with Patty about the move. The mother was responsive to the call and said they would talk that evening.

Follow-up

Pastor Carpenter was prepared to recommend family therapy for Patty if her problems continued, but when she checked back with Patty's teacher during the next few days he indicated that Patty was back to her old self. Patty's parents never called the pastor back, but at the parent-teacher conference three weeks later the teacher learned that they had talked at length that Tuesday evening at the supper table, and Patty did not seem to have any further problem.

Observations

Reviewing the case in the light of the A-B-C method, one can see that Pastor Carpenter had already apparently achieved a relationship with Patty, although no more than a few words each day had passed between them. The pastor had a natural ability for relating with children. Once she knew the facts she boiled down Patty's problem: "You feel bad because you don't have your same house or your same friends anymore," and "You are mad at your daddy for making the move." To the latter statement Patty had blurted out her definite response to the formulation: "Yeah!"

The pastor and the teacher mutually took responsibility for forming a method of action. They set up situations where Patty could not only talk about her loss but also receive the support of others. Because crises happen not only to individuals but also to families, they arranged for Patty to have a chance to talk about what was happening with her brothers first and then with her parents later the same day.

The teacher was very cooperative and empathetic in handling Patty. After becoming aware of Patty's problem, the parents were apparently also responsive to her feelings. The resolution of the crisis was worked out in a matter of hours, and Patty was back to her usual self thereafter.

These people in crisis represent a wide range of ages, backgrounds, abilities, and situations. But they share more than a casual observer might detect—a sense of loss or threatened loss, for example. And all responded to some variation of the crisis management strategies presented herein; all were returned to equilibrium and some even experienced emotional and spiritual growth as a result of the resolution of their crises.

SIX

The Church
as Caring Community

"Let us give thanks to the God and Father of our Lord Jesus Christ, the merciful Father, the God from whom all help comes! He helps us in all our troubles, so that we are able to help others who have all kinds of troubles, using the same help that we ourselves have received from God" (2 Cor. 1:3-4, Today's English Version). God's love for us is a prior condition for our loving others. The congregation is an instrument through which God's love is translated to those in need. As a caring community, the church is singularly well suited for responding to people in crisis.

THE CHURCH'S MINISTRY

Thomas F. McGee (Caplan 1964, 151), a mental health professional specializing in crisis work, describes four conditions essential for effective crisis intervention. The first is *location*. For crisis intervention to be effective, persons doing it must be involved with and located in a specific community; people in crisis—probably because of their paralysis, immobility, and difficulties in problem solving—rely upon helpers or agencies that are readily accessible.

Second is *availability*. Individuals in crisis must be able quickly to achieve contact with those who can help—during the period of crisis, not two or three weeks later; these moments of heightened psychological accessibility require less care or counseling effort than after the crisis triangle has tipped back to its base (see diagram 3 on p. 30).

A third condition is *mobility*. The counselor who sits in a mental health center waiting for people in crisis to show up is not able to take part in comprehensive crisis intervention. Those who help in crises must be able to go to the scene of a crisis, roll up their sleeves, and do what is needed—even to recognize and intervene in a crisis when no help has been requested.

Fourth, *flexibility of procedure* is needed. Crisis intervention requires a variety of means and methods, such as walk-in clinics, telephone calls, home visits, fifteen-minute supportive sessions, and use of paraprofessionals—as many resources and support systems as possible.

McGee's four conditions for effective crisis intervention are frequently better met by trained clergy and laypersons within the congregation than by the traditional mental health community. One of the chief advantages of the church in crisis intervention is its location. It has for centuries been known as the place where individuals in distress can go for sanctuary, for hospitality, and for help.

Associated with the building is not only its pastor but a whole system of concerned people who can be mobilized in a short period of time to care for others. From the standpoint of crisis intervention, this availability is a benefit because people in crisis generally can see the minister or a lay pastoral carer within a day or two, if not immediately.

The church as a community of saints has always been a movable institution. Ministers and laypersons can go to the scene of a crisis, whether it be an accident or disaster, a hospital room, a school, or the workplace. They are expected at the time of a death. The church's ministry is not closed up in the sanctuary but branches into the whole community. Christian fellowship has never been limited to a particular facility, but occurred from the beginning "where two or three are gathered in my name" (Matt. 18:20).

Mental health professionals are now beginning to realize the necessity of flexibility in procedure; at one time many therapists who thought they were very flexible and eclectic counselors did most of their counseling within the four walls of an office for fifty-minute sessions of face-to-face contact. They rarely took advantage of intervention methods that the church has historically used, such as home and hospital visits, letter writing or telephone calls, visitation by laypersons (paraprofessionals), and incorporation of the needy person into a group of caring individuals.

The purpose of the church is to increase and promote among all people the love of God and of each other. The church helps to communicate this love in a real and concrete way to individuals, so that they can respond to it with increased love for God and for one another. The three traditional tasks of the church have been defined as *kerygma* (teaching and proclaiming the gospel), *koinonia* (fellowship), and *diakonia* (implementing the faith in Christian love and service). Crisis intervention realizes all three forms of ministry. It proceeds primarily out of love and service (*diakonia*), but it also helps individuals relate better with others as a part of the community of God (*koinonia*), and it facilitates new learning (*kerygma*) at a time when people are especially open to hearing the Word. It is within the local church fellowship, and not only through the minister, that persons can come to know and care for one another in a way that makes genuine Christian community possible and stretches the pastoral care ministry beyond what the pastor does alone.

THE MINISTRY OF THE LAITY

The crisis caregiver does not have to be an ordained minister or a mental health professional. Laypersons doing crisis work are a natural extension of the church's network of care. Crisis centers and suicide prevention agencies have discovered the value of using volunteers from many walks of life—housewives, attorneys, construction workers—who are trained specifically in crisis intervention methods. The pastor who would extend the caring ministry of the local parish beyond what one person can accomplish can enlist and train many others to help in times of crisis.

One of the most beneficial ways of empowering members of the congregation in crisis intervention work is to gather a small cluster of lay pastoral carers and train them in intervention methods. Space here does not permit a detailed description of such a training program for lay pastoral care ministry; I have covered that subject in another book (Stone 1991). Such a training program should involve not only didactic input but also the use of role play, as well as teaching and practicing the A-B-C method of crisis intervention counseling. In this regard, the pastor can present typical cases (see chap. 4) for discussion in class. Role-play telephone intervention can be practiced by seating the participants back-to-back, thus preventing them from relying on facial or other visual, nonverbal clues.

Crisis lay pastoral carers can respond to the distinct needs of individual congregations, for example, by visiting the sick and shut-in, visiting after a death in a family, and visiting an extended care facility. Crisis lay caregivers can also be trained in general pastoral care visitation; they can develop and use their skills for helping shut-ins and others who are lonely but not experiencing a crisis.

Lay pastoral carers have an ongoing need for supervision and feedback. Supervision occurs best in a group setting, except in emergencies, when ministers can consult by phone or in person. Actually, crisis intervention training never ceases; but after the initial training sessions it changes from weekly classes to monthly supervision and ad hoc consultation. In discussing the training of paraprofessionals for crisis intervention, Edwin Shneidman (1973, 11) states, "What you need is a good heart, freedom from proselytizing for your own private causes, supervised training focused on crisis intervention, and a pinch of wisdom. . . . Three pre-conditions are essential: careful selection, rigorous training, and continuous ruthless supervision." For laypersons to function successfully as crisis interveners in congregations, ministers must not feel threatened by having people around them who are competent to do some pastoral care tasks. They must convey to the congregation that ministry is a function of the whole people of God, the priesthood of all believers. Every Christian is commissioned to care for others. The efforts of laypersons do not necessarily cut down on the amount of pastoral care visitation required of ministers—they may well increase it—but they can ultimately offer the congregation a broader-based, more inclusive pastoral care ministry.

The pastor and congregation can be involved in crisis work in a variety of ways. For example, members of the congregation can serve on the board of a mental health center. They can help encourage local crisis or mental health centers to be more effective and relevant to the community, offering help to all people and not just the privileged or the insured. Church people can establish and serve on hot lines or crisis intervention centers in communities where none presently exist. They can serve on existing crisis lines or other programs within the community that need volunteer help.

The group effort of a caring congregation for those in crisis can become an example of convergence behavior, a phenomenon that frequently occurs after natural disasters, in which there is an influx of people who are eager to help, looking for friends and relatives, or simply curious. Convergence behavior rarely occurs spontaneously in cases of emotional crisis, but in a congregation it can be fostered. Helpers engage anyone they can to meet the troubled persons' needs and to reassure them that they have not been abandoned.

Such deep genuine fellowship is an expression of koinonia. In the New Testament Paul speaks of the participation and mutual fellowship among believers, stemming from the relationship of each believer with the Christ. Koinonia is possible today among people who come together from all walks of life to share in one central concern. It is especially important in times of crisis, when a troubled person needs a sense of belonging and fellowship with other Christians.

One dimension of koinonia is partnership: all Christians are partners in Christ. Even in the pastoral care relationship, the helper and the helped alike give to and receive from each other. Koinonia is always active—never passive or stagnant. It is spontaneous and uncontrived; it is not inward but exists in relationships where sharing and reaching out occur; it is vigorous and honest and can involve—even require—encounters between people.

The potential for koinonia exists within all people. Out of it trust develops. As a result of it people can go to each other for succor in crises. Wherever koinonia exists within a Christian community, pastoral care naturally becomes a function of the entire congregation; people reach out to each other in their crises as well as in their day-to-day troubles, despair, hope, and joy.

Crisis intervention, whether undertaken by members of the congregation or the clergy, or both, is a core task of ministry aimed at encountering and caring for the many people in each community who experience crises. It is an important way in which Christians can express the love of God to persons at their times of greatest need.

Bibliography

Aden, L.
    1968   "Pastoral Counseling as Christian Perspective." In Homans, 163–81.

Bonhoeffer, D.
    1954   *Life Together*. Trans. John W. Doberstein. New York: Harper and Brothers.

Caplan, G.
    1964   *Principles of Preventive Psychiatry*. New York: Basic Books. Chapter 2, "A Conceptual Model for Primary Prevention," describes the characteristics of significant life crises and factors that influence their outcome.

Caplan, G., E. Mason, and D. Kaplan.
    1965   "Four Studies of Crisis in Parents of Prematures." *Community Mental Health Journal* 1(2):.

Childs, B.
    1990   *Short-term Pastoral Counseling*. Nashville: Abingdon Press. Excellent book on time-limited pastoral counseling.

Clinebell, H.
    1984   *Basic Types of Pastoral Care and Counseling*. Nashville: Abingdon Press. Chapter 8 suggests several different approaches to crisis counseling.
    N.d.   *New Approaches to Crisis Counseling*. Pastoral Care in Crisis Film Series. Distributed by Community Mental Health Services, Columbia, S.C.

de Shazer, S.
    1988   *Clues: Investigating Solutions in Brief Therapy*. New York: W. W. Norton.
    1991   *Putting Difference to Work*. New York: W. W. Norton.

Ellis, A. A., and R. A. Harper.
    1975   *A New Guide to Rational Living*. Los Angeles: Wilshire Book Co.

Erikson, E.
    1964   *Childhood and Society,* 2d ed., rev. New York: W. W. Norton.

Everstine, D. S., and L. Everstine.
 1983   *People in Crisis: Strategic Therapeutic Interventions.* New York: Brunner/Mazel.
Farberow, N., S. Heilig, and R. Litman.
 1968   *Techniques in Crisis Intervention: A Training Manual.* Los Angeles: Suicide Prevention Center, Inc.
Frankl, V.
 1963   *Man's Search for Meaning.* New York: Washington Square Press.
Fromm, E.
 1947   *Man for Himself.* New York: Holt, Rinehart and Winston.
Gerkin, C.
 1979   *Crisis Experience in Modern Life.* Nashville: Abingdon Press.
        An excellent book on a theological understanding of life crises.
Gilliand, B., and R. James.
 1988   *Crisis Intervention Strategies.* Pacific Grove, Calif.: Brooks/Cole.
        One of the best recent books on crisis.
Haley, J.
 1976   *Problem-solving Therapy: New Strategies for Effective Family Therapy.* San Francisco: Jossey-Bass.
Halpern, H.
 1973   "Crisis Theory: A Definitional Study." *Community Mental Health Journal* 9(4): 342–49.
Hauck, P. A.
 1980   *Brief Counseling with RET.* Philadelphia: Westminster Press.
Homans, P., editor.
 1968   *The Dialogue Between Theology and Psychology.* Essays in Divinity 3. Chicago: University of Chicago Press.
Jacobson, G.
 1965   "Crisis Theory and Treatment Strategy: Some Socio-Cultural and Psychodynamic Considerations." *Journal of Nervous and Mental Disease* 141(2): 214–15.
Jones, W.
 1968   "The ABC Method of Crisis Management." *Mental Hygiene* (January): 87–89.
Jung, C.
 1949   *Modern Man in Search of a Soul.* London: Routledge & Kegan Paul.
Kalicki, A., editor.
 1987   *Confronting Alzheimer's Disease.* Owings Mills, Md.: National Health Publishing.
Lazarus, R.
 1966   *Psychological Stress and the Coping Process.* New York: McGraw-Hill.

A ponderous but valuable volume that details a cognitive theorist's view of stress; discusses primary and secondary appraisal of perceived threat.

Lester, A.
1985   *Pastoral Care with Children in Crisis*. Philadelphia: Westminster Press.

Lester, D., and G. Brockopp.
1973   *Crisis Intervention and Counseling by Telephone*. Springfield, Ill.: Charles C. Thomas.

Mitchell, K., and H. Anderson.
1983   *All Our Losses, All Our Griefs: Resources for Pastoral Care*. Philadelphia: Westminster Press.

Oates, W.
1969   *Pastoral Care in Crucial Human Situations*. Valley Forge, Pa.: Judson Press.
        A helpful book that deals with such crucial concerns as mentally retarded children, chronically ill persons, and children with cancer.

Oden, T.
1986   *Crisis Ministries*. New York: Crossroads.

O'Hanlon, W., and M. Weiner-Davis.
1989   *In Search of Solutions: A New Direction in Psychotherapy*. New York: W. W. Norton.
        Although not a book on crisis intervention per se, it provides a good introduction to brief counseling.

Parad, H., editor.
1965   *Crisis Intervention: Selected Readings*. New York: Family Service Association of America.

Parad, H., and L. Parad, editors.
1990   *Crisis Intervention Book 2: The Practitioner's Sourcebook for Brief Therapy*. Milwaukee, Wis.: Family Service America.

Pastoral Psychology
1970   21 (April).
        The entire issue of this journal is devoted to the minister and crisis intervention; included are articles by G. Jacobson ("Crisis Intervention from the Viewpoint of the Mental Health Professional"), W. Morley ("Theory of Crisis Intervention"), and D. Switzer ("Crisis Intervention Techniques for the Minister").

Pittman, F.
1987   *Turning Points: Treating Families in Transition and Crisis*. New York: W. W. Norton.
        Provides a systems approach to handling crises that considers the impact of a particular crisis on the family as a whole.

Roach, M.
   1987   "Another Name for Madness." In Kalicki.
Roberts, A.
   1990   *Crisis Intervention Handbook: Assessment, Treatment and Research.*
          Belmont, Calif.: Wadsworth.
Rusk, T.
   1971   "Opportunity and Technique in Crisis Psychiatry." *Comprehensive Psychiatry* 12 (May).
Shneidman, E.
   1973   "Crisis Intervention: Some Thoughts and Perspectives." In Specter and Claiborn.
Specter, G., and W. Claiborn, editors.
   1973   *Crisis Intervention.* New York: Behavioral Publications.
Stone, H. W.
   1972   *Suicide and Grief.* Philadelphia: Fortress Press.
   1988   *The Word of God and Pastoral Care.* Nashville: Abingdon Press.
          Proposes a theological understanding of pastoral care ministry.
   1991   *The Caring Church: A Guide for Lay Pastoral Care.* Philadelphia: Fortress Press.
          The book describes a program of training laypersons in pastoral care.
   1993   *Brief Pastoral Counseling: Short-term Approach and Strategies.* Minneapolis: Fortress Press. Part One details approaches to short-term counseling; Part two coordinates specific strategies with typical presenting problems.
Stone, H. W., and W. Clements.
   1991   *Handbook for Basic Types of Pastoral Care and Counseling.* Nashville: Abingdon Press.
Switzer, D.
   1974, 1986   *The Minister as Crisis Counselor.* New York: Abingdon Press.
          An excellent volume covering all aspects of a pastor's intervention in the crises of parishioners.
   1989   *Pastoral Care Emergencies: Ministering to People in Crisis.* New York: Paulist Press.
Taplin, J.
   1971   "Crisis Theory: Critique and Reformulation." *Community Mental Health Journal* 7(1):13–23.

Index